COWB
Th

Edited & with an Introduction
by Virginia Bennett

Foreword
by Charlie Seemann

Illustrations
by Walt LaRue

Gibbs Smith, Publisher
Salt Lake City

3/05

First Edition

08 07 06 05 04   8 7 6 5 4 3 2 1

© 2004 Gibbs Smith, Publisher

Poems are reprinted by permission, and copyrights are held by the
authors or their estates.

Cover art © 2004 Buckeye Blake

Interior illustrations © 2004 Walt LaRue

Published by

Gibbs Smith, Publisher

PO Box 667

Layton, UT 84041

Orders: 1.800.748.5439

www.gibbs-smith.com

Designed by Meghan Merker

Printed in the United States of America

Library of Congress Cataloging-in-Publication Data

Cowboy poetry : the reunion / edited by Virginia Bennett;
foreword by Charlie Seemann. — 1st ed.
        p. cm.
Includes bibliographical references.
ISBN 1-58685-349-X
1. Cowboys – Poetry. 2. Ranch life – Poetry. 3. West (U.S.) – Poetry.
4. American poetry – West (U.S.) I. Bennett, Virginia, 1952 Feb. 18-
PS595.C6 C725 2004
811.008'0921636213 – dc22
                        2003020173

CONTENTS

Chapter 3: REFLECTIONS ON A LIFESTYLE

Chapter 4: FAMILY & the COMMUNITY OF COWBOYS

Chapter 4, continued:

Chapter 5: LOOKIN' BACK DOWN THE TRAIL

Chapter 6: CHARACTERS

ACKNOWLEDGEMENTS

I would like to thank the many poets who submitted their work for this collection. I received over a hundred poets' submissions. Each of these poets' work was worthy to be in this anthology. However, due only to space limitations, some are not included. There are far too many fine cowboy poets to be corralled into just one volume, and I encourage readers to seek out the work of all of these writers, who offer their own, unique perspective on ranching life.

Unless someone has a complete and exhaustive library of both classic and cowboy poetry, a collection such as this could not be accomplished without help. I thank Margo Metegrano at cowboypoetry.com for unending assistance, especially with the use of her online "anthology index." Tom Sharpe offered information on Henry Herbert Knibbs, Bruce Kiskaddon, and also with footnoting some terms. Utah poet Bob Christensen sent poems by the Holaday & Hampton Poet. Thoughtful assistance also came from Randy Williams of the Fife Archives of Utah State University.

Carmel Randle of Queensland, Australia, introduced me to the work of contemporary Bush poet Ellis Campbell, and also helped with defining Aussie terms. In addition, she provided background information on Banjo Paterson and Will Ogilvie. Waddie Mitchell,

Meg Glaser, and Linda Hussa supplied encouragement and words of wisdom. Bette Ramsey allowed me to use a rare, unpublished poetic piece from her late husband Buck's collection. Dave Stanley introduced, as ever, so many of us to the incredible work of Rhoda Sivell. Janice Coggin of Cowboy Miner Productions sent her press's compilation of Henry Herbert Knibbs' poetry. Cleo Hansen of the Western Folklife Center cheerfully provided any answer to any question. Jana Marck mailed a treasured copy of Wallace David Coburn's book, *Rhymes from a Roundup Camp.* Much appreciation is sent to my editor, Madge Baird, for her experienced eye, work ethic, and good humor. Thanks also to assistant editor Johanna Buchert Smith and book designer Meghan Merker for their keen attention to detail. And many thanks to Gibbs Smith for having the grand idea of producing a volume with one poem per poet, thereby allowing us to have a vast representation of cowboy poetry, past and present.

And to everyone who picked up the phone, wrote an e-mail or letter, gave advice or pointed me onto some new trail, I thank you for allowing me to be a part of your cowboy poetry family, and I'm looking forward to the next twenty years!

—*Virginia Bennett*

FOREWORD

In 1985, when a group of folklorists and cowboy poets got together in Elko, Nevada, for the first-ever Cowboy Poetry Gathering, they thought it would be a one-time event. Western Folklife Center Founding Director Hal Cannon had worked with state folklorists from western states and cowboy poets like Waddie Mitchell to identify active reciters and ranch poets throughout the West and bring them together in Elko. There were about forty poets, and the audience, mostly ranch families, numbered fewer than a thousand. Everyone, from participants to the media, loved the event, and the rest, as they say, is history. It was decided to have the event again the next year, and the next . . . and now, amazingly, we find ourselves celebrating the twentieth anniversary of what the United States Senate proclaimed "The National Cowboy Poetry Gathering" in 2000.

During those twenty years, the National Cowboy Poetry Gathering has grown into one of the West's premier cultural events. The Gathering sparked a grass-roots renaissance in western oral literature and music, inspiring some three hundred similar cowboy poetry and music events throughout the West in the past two decades.

This year, in 2004, as we reflect on this cultural phenomenon and look back over the past twenty years, we regret that many of the poets, musicians and friends who were there at the beginning are no longer with us. But we also see a new generation of young poets and musicians continuing in their footsteps, capturing in their work the contemporary experience of living and working on the land today. This anthology comprises some of the best of traditional cowboy poetry predating the present cowboy poetry "movement," as well as work created since 1985. It is a great retrospective, giving us a sense of where we have been and where we are going, and a fitting tribute to the men and women whose words reflect an authentic American West.

— *Charlie Seemann*
  Executive Director, Western Folklife Center

INTRODUCTION

There is a question often asked among cowboy poets and fans alike throughout the year as we look forward to that annual reunion known as the National Cowboy Poetry Gathering in Elko, Nevada. Wherever we might meet—at a festival in Wyoming, a ranch rodeo in California or eastern Oregon, or one of the hundreds of smaller "gatherings" held across the West, the question is almost always the same: "Will I see you at Elko?"

This event, which has become something of a global grange hall meeting, emerged in 1985 after a group of western folklorists, with Hal Cannon ridin' point, organized the first coming-together of cowboy poets. Gwen Petersen remembers her trepidation that first year: "Was I nervous when it was time to go on stage? Shoot, I don't remember. I think I was in a coma." When asked how many audience members attended, Gwen recalls that feeling of anxiety as a poet, about to share words from her heart for the first time, stands before a couple of hundred strangers: "How much audience showed up? I don't know, but there were a jillion or so."

Organizers chose the last weekend in January for their event, and I've heard it said that was done because those days would occur during a lull in work for ranchers. In truth, there is never a good time for a cowboy to leave his duties. Where we lived in the far north, cows were bred to calve in January and February so the calves would be large enough to make the arduous journey in July to the high country for summer grazing. And cowboys and ranchers need to be attentive during those weeks of calving. However, some folks found ways around minor problems such as these. They simply put their bulls in with their cows later in the year so their calves would be born after "Elko."

I was first invited to perform at the Gathering in 1990, and, as of this writing, have been back eleven times since. For me, the greatest gifts of those years have been the memorable friendships I've made. Friends like Jack Walther, an old-time cowboy and draft-horse teamster who I'd met in 1990 when we were both scheduled in a theme session at the Gathering. He later visited my family when we were holed up in a little travel trailer (employee housing!) on a ranch in central Oregon. He and his wife Irene entered the tiny steel tube that was our home, and sat elbow to cramped elbow in our "living room." True to form, Jack lightened the moment by saying, "So . . . what are you going to do with all this room?" Jack and I continue to write and call each other, and I have visited him and Irene at their ranch south of Elko. I would have never met someone like Jack, who ranches over a thousand miles from where I lived, if it had not been for the Gathering.

One year, while at the Gathering, I chatted with poet Paul Schmitt. He lived in western Nevada and we had not seen each other for a few years. He asked with eyes searching mine for sincere answers: "Virginia, how are you? Where are you and Pete living now? You know, sometimes, I am out on my horse or riding on the tractor and I find myself thinking, 'I wonder where Pete and Virginia are now and how they are doing.'"

This exchange prompted me to consider the treasure of these friendships we've made over time. I went home from the Gathering that year to the ranch my husband, Pete, managed in north-central Washington. As soon as I entered the house, I donned my old coveralls, snugged on a woolen cap, and with flashlight in hand, headed out to frozen pastures to check our calving cows. With the aurora borealis forming columns in the luminescent sky, words poured forth from my mind as I thought of all those close to us whom we miss.

> . . . *I will watch, with glances lingering, the rimrock trail*
>   *above my cabin*
> *And strain to see your silhouette against a midnight sky.*
> *I will bide, in expectation, to hear your bit-chains jingling,*
> *And hope to soon see northern lights reflected in your*
>   *horse's eye.*

The year 2004 marks the twentieth anniversary of the Gathering, and during that time we have become a family. We've watched children grow up, get married, and come back to the event with their own babies in their arms. Some couples parted ways, and on the other hand, many more were wed. We've buried friends too soon, and often worried, as we've said goodbye on that early Sunday morning, if we'd see that old-time pard again the next year. And, just as the listening audiences do as well, we go home thinking about the words we've heard in poetry and song, words that linger long after the last truck or bus has pulled out of Elko's Convention Center parking lot.

For cowboy poems have a life of their own. They are built with words that are spawned not only from labor, but also from an occupation with which the poet's very existence is expressly linked. A cowboy or rancher lives where he or she works, and what they do in their work determines their survival. Therein can be found the essence of cowboy poetry and the explanation for why its popularity only increases.

Let me share with you how I received the poems for this volume and how these words represent real lives. Nevada poet Deanna McCall mailed a letter with her poems, expressing worries over the effects of her area's drought and wondering if they would be able to hang on to the ranch. Dick Gibford of Bishop,

California, sent me his poems, handwritten on lined notebook paper, and since he did not possess a stapler, he clasped his treasured poems together with a safety pin through the binder-holes in the sheets of paper. Yula Sue Hunting's work came to me in script, written with a shaking, great-grandmother's hand.

Charlotte Thompson's poetry was accompanied by a letter that had been scrawled upon her lap as she and her husband, Dave, traveled over bumpy ranch roads to a cow sale, she with her treasured poems ready to be mailed as they passed a post office.

In my opinion, a cowboy poetry gathering's most important contribution has been the creation of a stage and audience for whom to present our words, and that sense of place has single-handedly nudged poets to produce thousands of pieces of work. Without an audience, without appreciation, the poet's interest dies, and with that, the genre withers as well. Fresh work flows freely after each gathering, where cowboys are newly inspired by the works of other writers, and charmed by appreciative listeners who return year after year to hear beloved poems, greet poets like longtime friends, and be enchanted by words that are attached to a life few know firsthand. Listen to poet Peggy Godfrey, a ranchwoman who lives and works on her isolated sheep and cattle ranch near Moffat, Colorado:

ELKO REFLECTIONS

The pain of parting

On Sunday

At Elko

Is like the drag

Of barbed wire

Across my hand

Or a paper cut

It brings the blood

To the wound

For days I bleed

Poetry.

We salute twenty years of kinship at Elko and at all the other gatherings across our land. We recognize the intangible bonds that will outlast even the events themselves, and we most of all laud the poets and the words that resound throughout the West, at campfires and festivals and within homes, bringing us smiles and tears forevermore.

— *Virginia Bennett*

CHAPTER 1

HOSSES

A cowboy or a cowgirl might live in Alberta or Arizona or any place in between. He might be leading a string of pack mules down into the Grand Canyon or up over the North Cascades in Washington State. She might be partnering on a ranch with her husband, ridin' eight hours gathering cattle, and cookin' for a roundup crew of twenty, all on the same day. Wherever you may find a cowboy or whatever he might be doing, you can be assured of one thing: horses are involved. Because without a horse, he just ain't a cowboy!

BUSTED

The Holaday & Hampton Poet (1878–1950)

Sometimes a hoss starts out all right.
He doesn't buck, he doesn't fight.
His back is mebby in a hump
But then he doesn't make a jump.

He starts off in a easy trot.
You think fer shore that he's forgot,
And keep a lookin' all around
Fer stock or signs upon the ground.

You jog along a couple mile;
He ain't done nothin' bad worthwhile,
You reckon ever thing's all right,
And ain't exactly settin' tight.

When all at once his head and ears
Goes onder him and disappears.
You ain't a settin' anywhere
But soter flying through the air.

He's throwed you on yore back and head,
You hit so hard you're must nigh dead.
You're weak and shook when you git up
And sicker than a p'izened pup.

You cuss him, but he's fur away,
He ain't a carin' what you say.
We've all done that. We've gone and trusted
A tricky hoss, and shore got busted.

Bruce Kiskaddon wrote many short poems under the pseudonym "The Holaday & Hampton Poet."

SQUALLIN' BALLEY & DIABLO

Wallace McRae

It's a story oft repeated in soulful cowboy rhymes:
"Old Squallin' Balley topped the ridge to that
   'Pasture in the Sky.'
He run off with my hobbles just one too many times,
Broke his neck in a fart knocker. Now angels sing
   his lullaby."

But the truth about some hosses is that they belong
   in hell
When their sneakin' sinful hearts pump that final beat.
And them lyin' rhymin' buckaroos know this fact
   full well
So their maudlin, soulful saccharine is chuck full of
   gross deceit.

See, I got this stumblin' knothead that's unsafe at
   either end,
When you're finally sittin' on him, he thinks, "It's
   temporary."
So just when you're relaxin' you'll come to
   comprehend,
As you're ascendin' and descendin', that you're no
   longer equestuary.

So I got this plan I'm workin' on when that sucker
      breathes his last.
I'll foller him, not up, but down to the sulf'rous
      range of hell.
And I'll ketch him up each mornin' 'n ride the
      outside circle—fast,
All cinched up way too tight, 'n never let him rest
      or blow a spell.

Cause all the grief that sumbitch has give me
      through the years,
Will sorta average out, while his spur-tracked sides
      are heavin'
As we're pullin' bog along the Styx as demon
      cavaliers
Hell, I'll spend eternity on old Diablo—gettin' even.

REMEMBERING
A MIDDLE-AGED BRONC RIDE

Rod McQueary

I sicc'ed him on a longhorn cow, tried to beat her
    down a hill,
I probably spurred too hard, the old dry cow had
    sure set sail.
Buckskin bronc forgot his manners, the way a
    bronco sometimes will.
When we jumped the bank, he came untrained,
    and ate his tail.

The first time I remembered it, I was on my
    hands and knees.
My hat was gone, blood dribbled off my chin.
I was slightly less than "pretty as you please,"
Contemplating this new shape that I was in.

I spit out a piece of barbed wire and what I hope
    was dirt.
I'd lost my cowbook, my pen and pencil set.
Waving gaily from a steel post was a big piece of
    my shirt.
My pelvis wouldn't hold me up, but I didn't know
    that yet.

When I stood up, I noticed a modest aching in
    my knee.
I must have kissed the cedar post, my glasses sure
    were bent.
I finally found my missing spur, hanging in a tree,
While I wondered where my buckskin buddy went.

He knows I enjoy a bronc ride, that's why he's so
    endeared.
He's so trustable, and cute, the little squirt.
But in case I might get cranky, he took my stuff,
    and disappeared.
I thought, "What a lovely time! I sure hope he's
    not hurt."

We found the buckskin, later, wandering aimlessly
    and loose.
We took him to the auction and, I hope,
He found a job that truly puts his talents to good use,
Like holding stamps upon an envelope.

Years pass.
Whilst trotting through my memories, this buckskin
    bronc showed up.
I thought of that sweet day we jumped the cow.
Now when it came to bucking, this buckskin was
    a pup.
I'd have no trouble staying on him—now.

You know, the day we chased that cow, I think
        I rode him pretty good.
I'm sure I gave the cowboy yell, and fanned his fat.
We nearly bumped a cedar tree, almost broke
        some wood.
That is probably why I dropped my hat.

It's been a while. The passing of, lo, these many days
Make those old, fond memories in my mind
Seem like ghosts. Appearing, sometimes, fading in
        the haze.
Precious as arrowheads. Sometimes, just as hard
        to find.

I remember riding some buckskin, spur rowels
        clogged with fur.
Spurrin', screamin', fannin' him, droppin' like a hawk.
He bucked down some hill, and jumped a fence,
        me clingin' like a burr.
This mid-aged-memory-losing myth is nothing but
        a crock.

I recall it now. That buckskin bucked downhill
        like hell.
He jumped a cliff, a tree, a fence. I rode him fine.
I almost lost my balance once, but never really fell.
You see, my memory's getting better all the time.

IF WE ALL RODE HORSES
LIKE THE ONES WE USED TO RIDE

Pete Bennett

Have you ever sat in camp
    attending a bull-slinging session?
It always revolves around those horses
    that used to be in our possession.
Why, there's nothing that any one of them
    critters could not do,
And the ramblin's go on with such gusto,
    you know they've got to be true.
These horses have somehow become exalted
    as names come up and stories are told.
More daring rides and deeds of greatness
    just naturally begin to unfold.
But there's just one thing I've noticed:
    those horses we're so quick to defend—
That when the subject is changed to bad broncs
    these same names will be brought up again!

Now, this really isn't meant to confuse you
    or make you feel like dudes,
It's just meant to show you
    that even the best horses do have moods!

Excerpted from Storms on the Divide, *self-published, 1991.*

THE RETIREMENT OF ASHTOLA

Larry McWhorter (1957–2003)

When a day's work is done in the limits of town
A man leaves his job at the site
Then he meets with his friends at their pet waterhole
To watch a big game or a fight.

But on the JA's when the saddles were stripped
And the pleasures of town far away,
They gathered 'round the chuckwagon fire
And recalled the events of the day.

Wild horses was rode and wide loops were thrown,
With no one missing, of course.
Then the tales of glory and daring died down
And Boy Blackwell was asked 'bout his horse.

Ashtola, the mount of this here account,
Was a legend who bore the famed brand.
This rider and steed were performers of deeds
That brought smiles from the hardest old hands

A big ol' gray horse who was honest of eye.
A range-wisened, crusty old bird,
And I've heard it said he'd not met the beast
That he couldn't put out of the herd.

A frustrated cow once used all her tricks
But Ashtola would thwart every plan.
Then she got him in close and a little sideways
So under his belly, she ran.

"A lot of horses would have lost her," Boy said,
"But Ashtola that cow didn't bother."
"Well, what did he do?" a big-eyed kid bit.
"Why, son, he went down there and got her!"

Such were the tales of this cagey old horse,
That's why he's remembered in glory.
I leave it to you as to whether it's true
But don't judge 'til you've heard all my story.

The years catch us all and it was clear late one fall
That Ashtola's long race neared its end.
So, he was given the heave. The JA he must leave
And ol' Boy must part with his friend.

Somehow that night a gate was left open
And Ashtola escaped in the night.
So when the truck from the soap factory came
The gray horse was nowhere in sight.

Boy turned him loose in a pasture he knew
That was remote and out of the way.
As he slipped off the rope and scratched 'tween his ears
To the tired old horse he did say,

"You'll not wash the face of some snot-nosed kid.
I'd never permit such a thing.
You spend your days in the ease that you've earned
And I'll see you come early spring."

That winter they had was the toughest in years
Five northers they seen that was blue.
So when the grass turned, with no small concern,
Boy rode to make sure he'd got through.

The canyons were bare, not a soul anywhere,
And he wondered, "Now where can he be?"
Then he noticed 'fore long that somethin' was wrong,
Neither cow nor calf did he see.

He topped out to look on a big flat below
Of the one corner he hadn't been
And the sight that he seen in that valley so green
Turned his worried frown into a grin.

Ashtola had throwed 'em all in a bunch
And was workin' the herd by hisself.
Then he thought of the years he'd spent on his back,
"That ol' horse never needed my help.

"Three cuts he had goin' and where he put 'em
    they stayed,
The cows with bull calves on the right.
The cows with heifer calves stood to the left,
But, boys, here's the curious sight.

"The third bunch was standin' way off to theirselves.
And I wondered, now what could they be?
So I eased down the hill for a closer look
And you'll never guess what I see."

The tension was high among the young bucks
As ol' Boy paused for what seemed like days.
"Well, what was they?" some big-eyed kid bit.
Boy grinned at him, then he said, "Strays."

Legends abound on the Goodnight range,
Some canyons are haunted, I've heard.
But the ghosts ceased their mischief and gathered
     to watch
When Ashtola was workin' the herd.

*According to legend, the horse in this poem could even
read the brands of cattle! Excerpted from* Contemporary
Cowboy Verse *by Larry McWhorter, published by
Cowboy Miner Productions, 2000.*

WALKIN' JOHN

Henry Herbert Knibbs (1874—1945)

Walkin' John was a big rope-hoss,
  from over Morongo way;
When you laid your twine on a ragin' steer,
  old John was there to stay.
So long as your rope was stout enough
  and your terrapin shell★ stayed on,
Dally-welte★ or hard-and-fast,
  it was all the same to John.

When a slick-eared calf would curl his tail,
  decidin' he couldn't wait,
Old John, forgettin' the scenery,
  would hit an amazin' gait;
He'd bust through them murderin' cholla spikes,
  not losin' an inch of stride,
And mebbe you wished you was home in bed—
  but, pardner, he made you ride!

Yes, John was willin' and stout and strong,
  sure-footed and Spanish broke,
But I'm tellin' the wonderin' world for once,
  he sure did enjoy his joke;
Whenever the mornin' sun came up
  he would bog his head clear down,
Till your chaps was flappin' like angel wings
  and your hat was a floatin' crown.

That was your breakfast, regular,
    and maybe you fell or stuck,
At throwin' a whing-ding, John was there
    a-teachin' the world to buck.
But after he got it off his chest
    and the world come back in sight,
He'd steady down like an eight-day clock
    when its innards is oiled and right.

We give him the name of Walkin' John,
    once durin' the round-up time,
Way back in the days when beef was beef
    and John, he was in his prime;
Bob was limpin' and Frank was sore
    and Homer he wouldn't talk,
When somebody says, "He's Walkin' John—
    he's makin' so many walk."

But shucks! He was sold to a livery
    that was willin' to take the chance
Of John becomin' a gentleman—
    not scared of them English pants.
And mebbe the sight of them toy balloons
    that is wore on the tourists' legs
Got John a-guessin'; from that time on
    he went like he walked on eggs

As smooth as soap—till a tourist guy,
    bogged down in a pair of chaps,
The rest of his ignorance plumb disguised
    in the rest of his rig—perhaps,
Come flounderin' up to the livery
    and asked for to see the boss:
But Norman he savvied his number right
    and give him a gentle hoss.

Yes, Walkin' John, who had never pitched
    for a year, come first of June.
But I'm tellin' the knock-kneed universe
    he sure recollected soon.
Somebody whanged the breakfast gong,
    though we'd all done had our meat,
And John he started to bust in two,
    with his fiddle between his feet.

The dude spread out like a sailin' bat,
    went floppin' acrost the sky:
He weren't dressed up for to aviate,
    but, sister, he sure could fly!
We picked him out of a cholla bush,
    and some of his clothes staid on;
We felt of his spokes, and wired his folks.
    It was all the same to John.

terrapin shell: slang for saddle

dally-welte: roping term, to take wraps around the horn
    after you rope an animal, rather than having the end of
    the rope tied "hard-and-fast" to the saddle horn

16

A SECOND CHANCE

Tim Jobe

In the Anacacho Mountains where the slick rock is
    the king
And the blackbrush and guajillo own the land,
A bay colt was born one morning by a barely
    flowing spring
On the Texas ranch of a shorenuff old cowman.

The man who owned the ranch was getting
    up in years
But he still held on and did the best he could.
He had two daughters, grown and gone:
    alone with all his fears
That he couldn't run the ranch the way he should.

So he started cutting back some, selling off
    some of his stock.
The broodmare band was the first to go.
They were gathered early autumn from their
    home out in the rocks
And hauled to the sale barn in San Angelo.

The bay was nothing special, just a raw-boned
    weanling colt.
He was separated from his mom and sold alone.
He was bought by a man that owned a ranch
    a few miles south of Holt,
Hauled to the ranch and kicked out on his own.

17

The man took ill right after that and had to move
    to town.
His banker son stepped in and took the ranch.
Just before the colt turned three, the banker eared
    him down;
Tried to ride him but he never stood a chance.

'Cause the colt was scared and angry, he did the
    only thing he could:
He bucked to get that demon off his back.
He dumped that ignorant banker; I mean really
    dumped him good
Then jumped the fence and made off with his tack.

He was branded as an outlaw and was hauled to
    town again.
He found himself in Wilson's bucking string.
They hauled him to some rodeos; he bucked good
    now and then.
He grew big and stout and quick and smart and mean.

But his heart just wasn't in it and one day he caught
    my eye.
I don't know why, just something that I saw.
There was something 'bout his look that said:
        If you'll give me a try
I could make a good cow pony after all.

18

So I bought him from the Wilsons and I hauled him
    to my spread.
I worked each day to build a bond of trust.
I gave him time to understand, to fix things in his head,
And decide if the things I asked of him were just.

It didn't take much time 'til he was giving all he could
To learn to do the things I asked him to.
He became an eager student, willing, kind and good.
I never found a thing he wouldn't do.

I've seen a lot of people who remind me of that horse.
They didn't get an even break on life.
Their circumstances somehow knocked them off
    the narrow course
And left them with a steady run on strife.

All they need's a different trainer to help them
    find their way.
Someone to take the time to lend a hand.
To show them how things ought to work,
    the way to earn their pay,
So they don't have to wear the outlaw brand.

HIS HORSES

Laurie Wagner Buyer

I do not dream of him or the way he once held me.
I dream of him and his horses—

their names sliding through fingers of consciousness
like butter-soft reins on a worn-out summer day—

Peanuts, Diamond, Blackie, Buck, Duchess, Claude,
Tequila, Bill, Honda, Shavano, Honeybee, Ned . . .

He swings a saddle, settles it on a humped-up back,
vapor puffs from flared nostrils as he reaches for the cinch.

He sticks a spurred boot into a stirrup and is gone,
riding into sunrise to chase down a herd of chores.

Slats, Socks, Smoke, Booger Red, Blue, Billy Bars,
Rastus, Poco, Wink, Jake, Keno, Dancer . . .

He heaves on harnesses, hames high over his head,
noses buried in grain boxes as he adjusts the britchin's.

Not easy to hold them, keep their heads up, his hands
slip on four-up lines stiff with twenty-below cold—

Pat & Mike, Stubby & Dick, Nell & Bell, Tom & Molly,
Donnie & Clyde, Jack & Jill, Hoss & Boss . . .

He counts wrecks the way some count birthdays,
each one a reminder that it's a miracle he's still alive.

I do not think of him and the way he once loved me.
I think of him and his horses—

their names echoing over the meadows as he stands
pitchfork in hand near the pole corral calling at dawn:

Amigo, Dunny, Brandy . . . Cookie . . . Candy.

SALLY

Tom Sharpe

Boss told me quite a story
'Bout what this mare could do.
But failed to mention her callin'
Was dog food, soap, or glue.

My elevator don't go plumb to the top,
And I'm one brick shy of a load,
So I never checked his story,
I believed what I was told.

Had to pull a foot up tight
To get her under the saddle,
But she never even tried to pitch
Once I got astraddle.

Fer packin' salt, she wasn't bad,
Just sort of like a sled.
Never had to trim her feet,
I'd drag 'em off instead.

Bears and steers were both the same
Inside her tiny brain,
Ride real close to either one,
She'd sull and act insane.

But we covered plenty miles
On that summer range,
Thought I had things going well,
She'd slowed in actin' strange.

'Til one day, in an oak brush patch,
She stepped down on a wire,
Then commenced to bust in two
Like her tail was set on fire.

We cleared an opening in that brush,
Then broke acrost a flat.
Her eyes were closed, she couldn't see,
An' going like a bat.

She was still buckin' hard
When that flat became a bluff,
Toe of my boot cleared the edge
Things was gettin' rough.

'Bout that time she hit a tree,
Right up side her head.
Stopped her pitchin', then looked up —
I prayed I wasn't dead.

I eased her back from that edge
And headed back to camp.
I just let her pick the way.
My pants was sorta damp.

Stole a ride back to home,
My soul was really shaken.
Wondered how I would explain
The life I'd soon be takin'.

Pulled my saddle with evil thoughts
Of how I'd cut her throat,
Then it came into my mind
How the boss had got my goat.

I let her be from that day on,
With hopes that she'd get fat.
Boss would need a horse sometime —
I'd tell him where she was at.

TEMPERED SOULS

Darin Brookman

I've seen the horses gamely trot
Defiant in the still.
With ears pricked up as if to test
The nerve in Nature's will.

I've seen the lightning bridge the gap
'Tween heavens and the sod,
Like careless insults tossed about
By some ill-tempered god.

I've heard the thunder roll across
The wide and lonely plain,
As to proclaim the coming
Of the driving, pelting rain.

Then in the keeping of the storm
I've stood with hobbled heart,
As things that man might build or plan
Were rudely torn apart.

But after each and every storm
In spite of what has passed,
I've watched in awe as new sun gave
The world a polished cast.

The ponies graze contented now
That storm on mem'ry's rolls.
Their backs still wet they carry on
With bruised but tempered souls.

THE PEARL OF THEM ALL

Will Ogilvie (1869–1963)

Gaily in front of the stockwhip
The horses come galloping home,
Leaping and bucking and playing
With sides all a lather of foam;
But painfully, slowly behind them,
With head to the crack of the fall,
And trying so gamely to follow
Comes limping the pearl of them all!

He is stumbling and stiff in the shoulder,
And splints from the hoof to the knee,
But never a horse on the station
Has half such a spirit as he;
Give these all the boast of their breeding,
These pets of the paddock and stall,
But ten years ago not their proudest
Could live with the pearl of them all!

No journey has ever yet beat him,
No day was too heavy or hard,
He was king of the camp and the muster
And pride of the wings of the yard;
But Time is relentless to follow;
The best of us bow to his thrall;
And Death, with his scythe on his shoulder,
Is dogging the pearl of them all.

I watch him go whinning* past me,
And memories come with a whirl
Of reckless, wild rides with a comrade
And laughing, gay rides with a girl—
How she decked him in lilies and love-knots
And plaited his mane at my side,
And once in the grief of a parting
She threw her arms round him and cried.

And I promised—I gave her my promise
That night as we parted in tears,
To keep and be kind to the old horse
Till Time made a burden of years;
And then for his sake and one woman's . . .
So, fetch me my gun from the wall!
I have only this kindness to offer
As gift to the pearl of them all.

Here! hold him out there by the yard wing,
And don't let him know by a sign:
Turn his head to you—ever so little!
I can't bear his eyes to meet mine.
There—stand still, old boy! for a moment . . .
These tears, how they blind as they fall!
Now, God help my hand to be steady . . .
Good-bye!—to the pearl of them all!

whinning: whinnying

EQUUS CABALLUS

Joel Nelson

I have run on middle fingernail
    through Eolithic morning
And I've thundered down the coach roads
    with the Revolution's warning
I have carried countless errant knights
    who never found the grail
I have strained before the caissons
    and moved the nation's mail

I've made knights of lowly tribesmen
    and kings from ranks of peons
and given pride and arrogance
    to riding men for eons
I have grazed among the lodges
    and the tepees and the yurts
I have felt the sting of driving whips
    and lashes, spurs and quirts

    I am roguish—I am flighty—
        I am inbred—I am lowly
    I'm a nightmare—I am wild—I am the horse
    I am gallant and exalted—
        I am stately—I am noble
    I'm impressive—I am grand—I am the horse

I have suffered gross indignities
    from users and from winners
And I've felt the hand of kindness
    from the losers and the sinners
I have given for the cruel hand
    and given for the kind
Heaved a sigh at Appomattox
    when surrender had been signed

I can be as tough as hardened steel—
    as fragile as a flower
I know not my endurance
    and I know not my own power
I have died with heart exploded
    'neath the cheering in the stands
Calmly stood beneath the hanging noose
    of vigilante bands

    I have traveled under conqueror
        and underneath the beaten
    I have never chosen sides—I am the horse
    The world is but a players' stage—
        my roles have numbered many
    Under blue or under gray I am the horse

So I'll run on middle fingernail
    until the curtain closes
And I will win your triple crowns
    and I will wear your roses
Toward you who took my freedom
    I've no malice or remorse
I'll endure—This Is My Year—
    I am the horse

RACEHORSE

Jess Howard

Joe showed up at the racetrack
   with a horse that sure could run,
An' when the dust had settled
   he had outrun everyone.

Record books were altered,
   famous bloodlines all took heed
Of a horse no one had heard of
   that was blessed with blinding speed.

Reporters cornered Joe inside
   a stall, an' closed the doors,
An' said, "We want the scoop
   on that amazing horse of yours."

"Tell me, sir, how old is he?
   An' where all's he been raced?"
Joe said, "He's eight an' up 'til now,
   He's not been anyplace."

The newsmen were all baffled
   disbelief was in the air.
"With speed like his, how come
   y' never raced him anywhere?"

Joe said, "I would of raced him,
   but speed's a tricky thing.
I couldn't catch the bugger
   'til he pulled up lame this spring."

WANDA JILL

Ellis Campbell

Now the stable door is sagging
    and its creaking hinges groan,
and the bridle-bit is rusting in its gloom.
And the wattles* sway in gorges
    where I rode you, gallant roan,
when the bluebell bush was bursting into bloom.

As you raced beside your mother
    with her coat of dappled grey,
and she shone beneath the morning's gleaming sun,
I remember fragrant blossoms
    and the scent of new-mown hay
and the creeping shadows when the day was done.

An upstanding, stylish filly with a nimble-footed gait;
rare intelligence and nature born to match.
Typical of Little Wonders—
    with the build to carry weight—
best among a likely season's well-bred batch.

Oh, we drafted cattle* often
    at the yards near Salmon's mill,
while the dust clouds swirled above the stockyard rail.
And your surging power thrilled me
    from the saddle, Wanda Jill,
as you snatched at snaffle-bit and martingale.

Nineteen years of faithful service
    on the Warragloaming plains,
where we mustered stock through spinifex and scrubs.
Battled droughts of blazing summers,
    swollen rivers when the rains
swept down gullies fringed with native saltbush shrubs.

Then we left behind the outback
    for a smaller farm in here,
where the distances were shorter when we rode.
And the stock were rather quieter,
    and the neighbours mostly near,
and the debt was somewhat smaller that I owed.

But the cattle's bellow drifting
    from the sheltered clump of pines
is less stirring than it was those days, somehow—
when your flashing hooves with nimble tread
    were crushing dandelions
as we raced to wheel a steer or wayward cow.

Now my aching joints are creaking
    and my hair is flecked with grey,
and your fretted bones are bleaching whiter still.
And the buttercups are wilting to salute a summer's day
where you rest among the bluebells, Wanda Jill.

wattles: trees that flower in the spring in Australia

drafted cattle: what American cowboys call "sorting cattle;"
    cutting certain cows out from the herd

Excerpted from The Gloss of Bush, *self-published.*

33

SPIRITS PURE

D. Enise and Debra Coppinger Hill

I could not see them, but I knew they were there,
the ground filled with thunder, shaking my soul.
From my safe place in hiding, up on the ridge,
strange, whispered callings told me to go.

At the edge, the whole valley, stretched out below;
I watched, enchanted . . . blood racing the wind.
My breath became theirs as they dashed into sight;
Wild hearts and hoof-beats charged around the bend.

I could smell the sweat as it ran off their bodies,
glistening on muscle as they ran towards the sun;
Knew without words their message and meaning,
they were Freedom, Truth and Love on the run.

The earth rose to meet me as they ran at full power,
hooves sent dirt sailing, in clouds towards the sky;
My heart pounded wildly in time with their thunder;
it filled me with joy . . . for with them, I could fly!

I still feel all around me, the wondrous splendor,
that took my breath as they came into sight.
The vision I witnessed, that day in the valley,
is the dream that I dream as I drift off each night.

Forever engraved on my heart and my memory;
Spirits so pure they were one with the earth;
They set me free in those magical moments,
their strength became mine in a glorious rebirth.

They say to touch Heaven, your soul must go higher,
to streets that are paved with gold and with pearls;
But for me, it's a ridge, high above an endless valley,
being one with the horses, at the top of the world.

Excerpted from Mustangs the Evolution, *published by Old Yellow Slicker Productions.*

RIDIN'

Charles "Badger" Clark (1883–1957)

There is some that like the city
Grass that's curried smooth and green,
Theayters and stranglin' collars,
Wagons run by gasoline.
But for me it's hawse and saddle
Every day without a change,
And a desert sun a-blazin'
On a hundred miles of range.
Just a-ridin', a-ridin'—
Desert ripplin' in the sun,
Mountains blue along the skyline—
I don't envy anyone when I'm ridin'.

When my feet is in the stirrups
And my hawse is on the bust,
With his hoofs a-flashin' lightnin'
From a cloud of golden dust,
And the bawlin' of the cattle
Is a-comin' down the wind,
Then a finer life than ridin'
Would be mighty hard to find.
Just a-ridin', a-ridin'
Splittin' long cracks through the air,
Stirrin' up a baby cyclone,
Rippin' up the prickly pear as I'm ridin'.

I don't need no art exhibits
When the sunset does her best
Paintin' everlastin' glory
On the mountains to the west.
And your opery looks so foolish
When the nightbird starts his tune,
And the desert's silver-mounted
By the touches of the moon.
Just a–ridin', a–ridin'—
Who kin envy kings and czars
When the coyotes down the valley
Are a-singin' to the stars, if he's ridin'?

When my earthly trail is ended
And my final bacon curled
And the last great roundup's finished
At the Home Ranch of the world,
I don't want no harps nor halos,
Robes nor other dressed-up things.
Let me ride the starry ranges
On a pinto hawse with wings!
Just a–ridin', a–ridin'—
Nothin' I'd like half so well
As a-roundin' up the sinners
That have wandered out of hell, and a-ridin'.

This poem first appeared in the August 1906
Pacific Monthly.

A GOOD ONE

Wylie Gustafson

There's nuthin' like a good one between yer knees
Light to the rein and willin' to please
Together as one the day will be done
On a good one, I'll find my way home.

The world looks better from up on a throne
Strapped to the topside of muscle and bone
Below me, a friend, on whom I depend
On a good one, I'll find my way home.

Where luck is fickle and the days are long
Danger is quick and the cattle are strong
Married in movement, purpose and song
On a good one, I'll find my way home.

When at last the angels call my name
And the trail is ended on this earthly plane
Just carry me away on a big, honest bay
On a good one, I'll find my way home.

CHAPTER 2

JEST FER
THE FUN OF IT

When you live every day where the harsh and cruel sides of Nature are often seen . . . where the weather report is not just what you hear on the evening news but the environment in which you must get your job done . . . where you labor your entire life without a retirement plan or hope of a pension and you work with unpredictable animals, old equipment, and cranky hired hands . . . well, it's pretty hard not to have a good sense of humor!

Enjoy these fun-loving storytellers who, within their own communities, are the first to be invited to picnics, campfires, and socials just for their abilities to spin a tale or tell a wild yarn.

A DIFFERENT POINT OF VIEW

Dennis Gaines

"What a satisfying life you have," said the blue-haired
    matron,
Who'd bestowed her gracious company upon the
    wagon patrons.
The punchers stood politely by and listened to her spiel,
Which she delivered ardently with city-woman zeal.

"The clean, fresh air, the open skies, in touch with
    Nature's charms,
And nurturing God's creatures while preserving
    them from harm.
What joy is yours to birth a calf and watch him
    grow to health!
Your rewards are so much greater than the tawdry
    trap of wealth."

But she twisted diamond rings upon her fingers
    as if vexed,
And posed a careful question in a voice that was . . .
    perplexed.
"How can you dedicate your lives to keeping harm
    at bay,
Yet bring yourselves to dine on beef three times or
    more a day?"

The boys all cut their eyes, and with unanimous
    acclaim
They threw it to the wagon boss; Turk Harney was
    his name.
Harney wasted little time declarin' he'd consider
That there ain't no greater misery than tendin'
    bovine critters.

"There's just two things they're meant to do: that's
    die an' run away,
And I won't pretend to like 'em 'til my bones are
    in the clay.
They'll drool an' puke an' defecate an' cause undue
    distress,
An' cause heathens just like me to get religion
    an' confess."

"So it should come as no surprise what I'm about
    to tell,
An' if it's a mortal sin I know I'll gladly burn in hell.
There's no monumental mystery like them boulders
    at Stonehenge.
Ma'am, I don't even like the stuff—I eat it for revenge!"

Excerpted from New Tradition: Western Verse,
published by Teepee City Productions.

THE PARROT

Dallas McCord

It was time to hire a new camp cook,
The old camp cook had died.
He had cooked at the ranch for twenty years
With his parrot by his side.

At cookin' and bakin' and fixin' beans
No one could hold his pot.
But he also taught that bird to cuss
'Cause, ol' Cookie, he cussed a lot.

That parrot could cuss a blue streak;
He knew every foul word in the book.
And this didn't endear him to Chester.
You see, Chester was the new camp cook.

He worked for hours every day
To teach non-cuss words to that bird.
But every hour of every day
The cussing was the worst he'd heard.

One day, he grabbed that cussing bird
And tossed him in the shed.
But the cussing got so mean and foul,
Ol' Chester just wished he were dead.

He couldn't shoot or smash the thing.
After all, it had been there for years.
But the language spewing from its beak
Could drive a sailor to tears.

But finally, Chet had heard enough.
He didn't want to hear any more.
He threw the bird into the freezer
And then he slammed the door.

Well, all was quiet as seconds passed.
Chet opened the door for a peek.
The parrot was standing quietly now,
Not offering to move or speak.

So, then ol' Chet, he extended his hand and
The parrot stepped on with cold feet.
Chet returned him to the perch
With no cussing, no squawk and no tweet.

Finally, the parrot spoke up and said,
"Ya know, I'm sorry for cussing at you.
And I'm turning over a whole new leaf.
So, what'd those chickens do?"

THE CHRISTIAN HORSE

Howard Norskog

I called old Buck the Christian horse.
You'll wonder why I say,
But every time I stepped aboard
That's when I learned to pray.

I think the good Lord sent him down
For sinners just like me,
'Cause you'd take the path to righteousness
As you'd mount up, you see.

Now, if you just don't understand
Too much about God's wrath,
Just get yourself a Christian horse;
He'll get you on the path.

'Cause when you're finally mounted,
These words you'll say, of course:
"Dear Lord, if you can't help me now,
Please God, don't help this horse!"

RECIPE FOR ROUGH

Dee Strickland Johnson

A little boy climbed on his grandfather's knee,
Said, "Grandpa, how come you're so tough?
You rope and you ride, and you chew on rawhide.
What makes you so rugged and rough?"

The old cowboy grinned, said, "I'll let you in
On my little secret for roughness:
Gunpowder on oatmeal for breakfast each day!
That's sure to assure tough-enoughness!"

Well, the little boy did as his grandpa had said,
Gunpowder for breakfast is great!
He died hale and hearty at his own birthday party
At the age of one hundred and eight.

He left seventeen kids, forty grandkids,
Sixty-seven *great*-grandkids in all;
Also left, when he died, a hole fifteen feet wide
In the thick crematorium wall.

DOCTORING WORMS

Georgie Sicking

You have had some stormy weather
Some good old summer rain.
The grass is draggin' on your stirrups
And cattle on the gain.

The rock holes where the cattle water
Are full and runnin' over.
At first glance it looks
Just like everything is clover.

Then you spy a droopy-looking calf
Standing there and then he turns.
You might as well get your rope down,
That dogie is full of worms.

You ride up on him sort of easy,
Your horse is walkin' slow.
You build your loop just right
And catch him the first throw.

You would surely hate to chase him
Because he has got 'em pretty bad.
He is weak and kind of little
And lookin' mighty sad.

Then the cook has Spanish rice for supper
And it makes your stomach squirm
After ridin' in the summertime
And doctorin' a case of worms.

Excerpted from Just Thinkin', *published by Loganberry Press.*

CHARLOTTE'S COW

Charlotte Thompson

Some people say and believe it:
A cowboy won't milk a cow.
No self-respecting buckaroo
would ever even know how.

But we live far from town and have children,
and fresh milk's so handy,
so Dave brought me in an old range cow . . .
well, it took Dave, Loy and Andy.

They left her tied to a gatepost,
pawing and kicking the dirt,
said, "Well, she's yours, Ma.
Now, be careful that SHE don't get hurt!"

I went to the house for a bucket,
a coffee can was all I could find,
and when I got back, boy, she was mad,
this gentle old milk cow of mine.

I built me a loop for her feet then,
and finally I did catch just one.
One of my boys jumped down from the fence
and said, "Boy, Mom, ain't we having fun?"

With his help I dallied her back foot
across to the other gatepost.
By now I was starting to wonder
just who really wants this milk the most.

Now she was more than just angry,
and she threw herself on the ground.
So I lay across from behind her
and milked my old cow upside down.

We've had her in for a week now
and she's gentled down just a tad.
But when I come out with my coffee can
she still paws the ground and gets mad.

One thing I know and it's certain,
a cowboy won't milk, not a chance.
The reason why I'm so certain:
It's the most dangerous job on the ranch!

Excerpted from Cowboys of Nevada: Poetry by
Charlotte Thompson, *published by Sweet June
Publishing.*

JUST HAD TO RUN AND ROPE HIM

R. W. Hampton

I just had to run and rope him.
Seemed like the thing to do.
Old Grey was feelin' corn-fed good.
Had me a new rope, too.

And sometimes the fever takes a man;
he fails to stop and think.
Why, to see those slick ears through the brush
is like a poison drink.

I just had to run and rope him,
and you'd think I'd know enough—
I went and roped that wild cow brute
and never did cinch up.

I just had to run and rope him,
a damn fool thing to do.
That maverick wears my brand new rope,
my Bob Marrs saddle, too.

And Old Grey, he lit out for the ranch,
a-leavin' me out here,
afoot in this mesquite patch,
cold-trailing that derned steer.

I just had to run and rope him
and although I could be pissed,
it weren't that bad as I look back.
At least I didn't miss!

SMALL TOWNS

Ed Brown

Just a nosy, bossy spinster
Allergic to all fun
Her life's devotion: GOSSIP
Every town's got one

Just last week my truck was parked
In front of our one bar
Miss Busybody saw it
Amongst the other cars

So my status has been altered
"The town drunk" now I'm called
With gossip, instant, lightning speed
The whole town knows it all

What goes around then comes around
I didn't want to fight
So I just parked my pickup
In her driveway all last night

OUR 10TH ANNIVERSARY

Echo Roy-Klaproth

This morning when he bellered out, "Cut 'er,"
I watched a fat, ten-year-old dry saunter
down the alley, oblivious to her fate;
but I took it personally, givin' her the gate.
From an era past, our Hereford hold-out,
a good mama cow without a doubt,
never sloughed a calf,★ a faithful ole girl—
and he was cuttin' this valuable pearl?

The next ten or twenty came pressing by
with nary a word from him—and why?
They were younger and from a fancy breed:
producers—that's what today's ranchers need.
'Twas later that night I swallowed the lump
when I felt the gentle pat on my rump
and heard, "Thanks for your help today, my dear.
I think that I'll keep you another year."

★*sloughed a calf:* miscarried

*On a ranch, cows are pregnancy-tested after breeding,
and usually the ones found "open," or not pregnant,
are "cut" from the herd and sold.*

DILLY WAH DILLY

Paul Steuermann

Several years ago in ol' Montan'
My horse-trading days had just began
And I asked a guy about a horse one day.
He said, "Son, he's a DILLY WAH DILLY from
    CHICKY WAH SHAY."

I said, "What the sam hill are you talking about?
I've never heard a description like that come out
Of a cowboy's mouth. And just to be sure
I think you should tell me a little bit more."

He said, "It's an expression of honor and it's only
    bestowed
On the finest horses that's ever been rode.
And if that description is not said in jest
Then you know that you're buying the very best."

So I bought his horse 'cause I believed what he said
And I stepped up on him and gave him his head
Man, I'm proud as could be as I rode away
On that DILLY WAH DILLY from CHICKY WAH SHAY.

My travels took me south towards the Mexico line,
And that expression I'd heard had plumb slipped
    my mind.
I was buying horses for the U Bar brand
Way down in Arizona in the cactus land.

My order for horses was just about filled
When I spots this caballo and I sure liked his build.
"You don't want him," I heard the foreman say.
"He's a DILLY WAH DILLY from CHICKY WAH SHAY."

I figured I'd put the foreman to the test.
I said I thought that expression was reserved for
    the best.
He looked at me with that sunburned grin
And said,"Kid, that title is worse than sin.

"Only the baddest of the bad is given that name.
You may not want my advice, but just the same:
Beware of a horse that's titled like that
Because he'll kill you, son, just as quick as a cat."

Well, I'm kinda confused and I don't understand
The difference of opinion in this southern land.
So I gathered my horses and got them away
From that DILLY WAH DILLY from CHICKY WAH SHAY.

I headed back north and in Nebraska I'm found.
I'm still buying those horses from folks all around.
When I spied a beauty that set my heart awhirl.
It's the flower of my dreams. Good God, it's a girl.

Well, I don't mess around. I prances right up.
I'm gonna drink my fill from that loving cup.
I'm aiming at marriage, but I'm not sure how,
Then she said, "Come on, cowboy. There's no time
    like now."

It happened real fast and soon we were wed.

Then my hands got sweaty and I got light in
the head,

Because I remembered the words I heard her
father say,

"She's a DILLY WAH DILLY from CHICKY WAH SHAY!"

Excerpted from Pure Pony Marbles, *self-published.*

OL' SMOKE

Jeff Streeby

We onct had a dawg an' we called 'im ol' Smoke.
He'as old, fat, an' lame an' 'is teeth 'as all broke.
He'as lazy an' ugly an' mean as a snake—
He'd bin raised up an' trained by my great uncle Jake.

A long time ago, when he'as reckless an' young,
He'as a bonified stock-workin' son-of-a-gun—
A bob-tailed, jaw-snappin', kick-duckin' rip-snorter
With 'is teeth in their noses er their heels
    er their quarters.

He'as spiteful o' sheep an' he'd steal the odd chicken.
The pups on the place all knowed he could lick 'em.
Wherever he walked he'as top dawg in the yard
He din't mess with no cows 'cause he 'as re-tared.

Well, he hated the mailman an' he hated all kids—
He just hated all people, whatever they did.
He hated the preacher an' he hated my ma,
But, somehow, he got on purty good with my pa.

Still, out in the pastures 'mongst the mares an'
    the foals
You'd a' swore all his vileness had mellered to gold.
He'as like to a angel er a holified saint.
It ain't somethin' that's easy to figger, it ain't.

His ways, they'as legend where we lived way out
     there—
Not the spookiest colt er the worst foal-proud mare
Would lift a foot, roll a eye, er lay back their ears
'Cause they knowed that ol' Smoke, he weren't
     nothin' to fear.

He'd sit 'im right down in the shade 'tween their
     feet
An' he'd chew off their chestnuts★ like they'as a
     treat.
He'd nip 'em an' bite 'em an' nibble an' chaw—
It'as the gol-dangedest thing I ever have saw.

We'd see 'im out there on 'is afternoon stravage.
You'd nivver suspect he'as such a sour ol' savage.
The foals would all foller like a long string
     o' ducklin's
An' him in the lead just a-towin' them sucklin's.

He slept in a hole he'ad dug in the yard.
When the mail come one mornin', weren't no
     Smoke on guard.
He'as dead by the apple-tree, 'longside o' the porch.
Time an' plain orneriness jus' put out 'is torch.

We buried 'im then, right there where he died.
Wrapped 'im up in ol' horse blankets. Even Pa
     cried.
Fer a month after that the foals all milled around
At that spot in the fence where he 'ad started
     'is rounds.

Even now, the old mares, under afternoon skies,
Stop what they're a-doin' an' turn up their eyes
Toward that apple-tree a-growin' 'longside
    o' the house,
Like they'as a-waitin' fer that ugly ol' dawg to
    come out.

Well, he's under them apple-boughs an' safe from
    abuse,
But them apples is too sour now to be o' much use.

chestnuts: horny growth on the inside of each of a horse's
    four legs.

*This poem is about a dog that belonged to a First Sergeant
in the Fourth Cavalry when it was stationed at Camp
Dodge in Des Moines, Iowa. Excerpted from* The Wild
Crew: Riders and Horses, *published by Cavvyard Press,
2001.*

VERA

Carmel Randle

In a lonely Outback homestead
  Quite remote from City life
Lay the station-owner★ dying—
  By his side, his loving wife.

And he tried to speak a little,
  So she bent her head to hear—
"Remember when I met you, Vera?"
  "Yes, I remember, dear."

"I didn't have a penny, but
  You loved me just the same,
And one fateful winter's evening
  You agreed to take my name."

"Yes, dear! I remember that!"
  His loving wife agreed.
"Then you came out here, and worked so hard
  To fill my every need.

Depression brought us hard times—
  But you stood here by my side
Through the drought of nineteen-thirty-two
  When all our cattle died.

But Vera, you were always there!"
   She quietly said, "That's right."
"And even when I went to war—
   You didn't want to fight

But you joined the nursing service
   And were always near at hand
To lend support!" She quietly spoke,
   "I'm glad you understand!"

"Then back here on the property
   We reared our only child,
But we lost him, Vera—lost him!"
   "Yes, I know," she sadly smiled.

"Now the bank is taking over
   And there's one thing that I grieve—
I've worked so hard so many years
   But I've nothing much to leave!"

"Don't worry now, my darling!
   Some dreams do come unstuck!"
"You know what, Vera?" "Yes, Darling?"
   "I think you're bloody bad luck!"

*station-owner: in the Outback of Australia,
   a "station" is a stock ranch.

Excerpted from Gone Bush!, *self-published, 1996.*

CHAPTER 3

REFLECTIONS ON A LIFESTYLE

Men and women of today's West write eloquently of their surroundings: the animals that share their days; the honor integral to the cowboy spirit; the misfits we all know and love; and just a simple day in September when the light first changes to sparkling Autumn.

THAT "NO QUIT" ATTITUDE

Waddie Mitchell

While gathering cattle near the ruins
    of a long-abandoned homestead,
in the shadows of the mountains,
    questions swarmed around my mind
of the people who had claimed there,
    most forgotten now and long dead.
Still, I wondered what had prompted them
    to leave their world behind,

Searching for a life uncertain
    in this vast and rugged region,
up and leave their home and kin
    for opportunity to find,
taking little more to start with
    than an idea and a reason,
and the dream of their succeeding
    in a future yet defined.

Soon, these queries led to more, like
    why it is that some folks always
need to push their borders out beyond
    the farthest milestone
on some never-ending quest to find
    new ways and trails to blaze
and, in the process, stretch the realm
    of what is built and done and known.

From a little draw above me,
     in my pard rides with his findin's,
throwing his bunch in with mine,
     now shaded up and settled down.
I could see he'd gone through battle,
     for his pony's sportin' lather,
but his smile claimed he'd made it in
     with everything he'd found.

The sweat and dust and brush streaks
     on that pair done heaps o' speaking
as he pulled up near, dismounted,
     loosened latigo a bit.
Said, "We jumped 'em in the roughs
     and would've lost 'em had we weakened,
but, I swear, this here caballo
     ain't got one half ounce of quit."

And that "no quit" phrase speaks volumes
     on one's character and makin's
to the cowboy drawin' wages,
     ridin' ranges of the West.
Those who have it, you'll find usually
     conquer most their undertakin's
for the best in them is drawn out
     when their spirit's put to test.

Then, I spot my cowdogs brushed up,
     stayin' well-hid from the cattle,
knowin', with a cue, they'd give all
     to do anything need done.
And I thought then how the most of us
     will opt to shun that battle
never knowing fully what we could
     accomplish or become.

Still, I believe, like dogs and horses,
    we're all born with resolution
and, like muscles and good habits,
    it needs use and exercise.
When left dormant, it's in jeopardy
    of loss to evolution,
for eventually, it shrivels up
    in atrophy and dies.

But when flexed, it blossoms heroes
    and a source of inspiration,
for we all recognize the virtues
    in a "no quit" attitude.
And it proves its attributes
    in competition and vocation,
which evokes appreciation
    and a show of gratitude.

And since mankind started walking,
    it's been swifter, higher, stronger,
as if pushed by some deep need
    to keep their limits unconfined.
Almost thriving, always striving
    for things bigger, better, longer
in some unrelenting pursuit
    of perfection redefined.

Yet, in this world of soft complacence,
    there's still a few among the masses
who will readily give all
    to see a job or dream fulfilled.
It's a trait that's void of prejudice
    toward races, sex or classes,
just demanding its possessor
    be of valor and strong-willed.

Then, as we point our cattle homeward,
    lettin' dogs bring up the rear,
and we leave what's left of, once,
    somebody's hopes and dreams behind,
I'm convinced that "no quit" attitude
    will always persevere,
and that's the essence and the promise
    and the crown of humankind.

Waddie was commissioned by the Olympic Committee to write a cowboy poem for the official program of the Salt Lake 2002 Winter Olympics. This is the result.

OH ~ YOU ~ COWBOYS!

Sally Harper Bates

Oh ~ you ~ cowboys!
You know you've lived the life!
You ran the ridge at evening tide
And watched the daylight fade.
You climbed the hill at break of day
And breathed the crispy air.
You ran loose horses thru the grass
And smelled the broken stems
While a summer storm came rollin' in
With the sweetest scent on earth.
And you rode the range where life was found
In a simple bovine birth.
You stood on the porch with a coffee cup
That steamed in frozen air
While you watched a kid just learnin' the ropes
Run the dusty remuda in.
You rode the broncs and the solid mounts
And the one who chinned the moon.
You smelled the air as clean and fresh
As any that blows the earth.
You sat your horse on the crest of hills
Where the lupine blossomed free
And no other man had set his boots
Since maybe time began.
You rocked along at an easy lope
While the leather creaked out loud
And your rowels sang with the beating sound

Of hoofbeats on the ground.
Oh ~ you ~ cowboys . . .
Oh you horseback men!
You lived the life of kings astride
And watched the moon fall down.
No wonder the world would envy you
For a drink of freedom's cup.
Oh ~ you ~ cowboys.

PRAYERS

Deanna Dickinson McCall

We prayed for rain, prayed for snow
The prayers were but an empty echo
Returning to taunt again and again
As springs dried and cattle grew thin.

Searching for cattle, searching for feed
On horses weary and weak-kneed
We became gritty, dry as the land
Cracked and parched as the blowing sand.

We watched clouds gather, and gather more
Shadows darkening the valley floor
Followed by silence so profound
Shattered by drops striking ground.

We shouted for joy, shouted for fear
As sounds of thunder drew near
Lightning came in its wake
Unfurling like a blacksnake.

We saw it strike, and strike again
Smelled the smoke on the wind
Heard the wind lift and rise
To help her ally from the skies.

The grass burned hot, and hotter still
A red swath cutting down the hill
Consuming all in its path
Exploding trees in its wrath.

We spurred our mounts, and spurred again
Driving cattle before the wind
Blindly whirling in the smoke
Every breath a ragged choke.

The heavens opened, and opened wider
Drenching every cow and rider
Dry earth became a quagmire
As death was dealt to the fire.

We climbed the ridge, climbed some more
Turned to look through the downpour
As the fire gave a final roar
Lay smoldering on the valley floor.

Cattle were counted and recounted
While the knots in our bellies mounted
We were short, out a few
But we had done all we could do.

We pushed the cattle and pushed them more
Their sorry hides scorched and sore
On horses cloaked in suds and sweat
Knowing God's wrath we had met.

We watched the skies clear, and clear again
And hung our heads with the sin
Of our answered prayer that day
And watched our storm drift away.

THE SOUND OF SPURS

Dick Gibford

The sound of rushing water
And long grass combed by the wind,
The sigh of the pine on the mountainside
Remind me of dear old friends.

And the sigh'n' of a lover,
Her long hair a-fallin' down,
Her silken lips and the warmth of her hips
Draw me back to town.

In her luxury there, I will stay
Maybe a day or two,
Where what I knew seems so far away:
The lonely life of a buckaroo . . .

But a few more days in this dreamy haze
And I miss the horse and saddle.
It seems so strange, but I miss the range,
The wild bronc and stubborn cattle.

So, I quietly leave before there is time to grieve
Or dwell on those eyes of hers,
For what I miss with zeal is the booted heel
And cheery sound of spurs.

PRIESTS OF THE PRAIRIE

Linda M. Hasselstrom

Whispering practical prayers for the dead,
the brotherhood meets in choir.
Girdled in righteousness, bony backs straight,
circling the funeral pyre.
Their dusty black tunics hang flat on their bones,
shoulder to shoulder they stand.
Tonsured heads wobble on scraggly necks
as they pray in the pastureland.
From out of the west, the priesthood has come,
cloaks shining black in the sun,
to gather around this altar of flesh
until their communion is done.
Their eyes see forever — and somewhat beyond;
eternity, and a square meal.
The Brothers of Buzzard are worshiping lunch,
devouring the finest of veal.

PHOTOGRAPHER'S EYE

Barney Nelson

about the end of September
sunlight begins to look crisp
instead of mellow
the sun
I know
can't suddenly change angles
the earth can't suddenly tilt
but light changes
and it happens one day
in the fall
I know
leaves cut off
the food supply to trees
— or vice versa
perhaps the change
in light
happens on the day
when leaves stop absorbing
and begin to reflect
scientifically
I can't explain
I don't know
but some hot green fall afternoon
I will stop to water my horse
step off to soak a twisted cotton bandana
in the spring and tie it dripping

around my neck
to let
trickles
and faint breeze cool my skin
tuck a stray strand of grey hair behind my ear
and notice
the silver sparkle in cottonwood leaves

ONE MOMENT, PLEASE!

John Dofflemyer

In these hills, a man finds space that feels
familiar and friendly, and it must ask
in ways where we hang empty words
like ribbon just to find our way back—but
we stay a moment and let our horses blow.

They feel it—perhaps they feel it first
and do the asking of the place, or perhaps
it is the shards of light diffused at dawn
upon the many-legged oaks standing
knee-deep in grasses on the near ridge

that shield us from man's square creations,
his cubic thinking. Perhaps the sensual grace
of limb or slope, or granite worn to look
inside our minds, but there are places
that ask nothing else of us but to breathe

and taste the air, inhale with our eyes
and drink with our flesh for just a moment.
Once dared, it becomes ever easier to be
enveloped with the wild, an addictive peace
that embraces awe as eagerly as a child

might love—where a man can ride beyond
his time and station, beyond the tracks of those
before him: spaces that beg a moment's notice
where both grand and simple revelations
are left and learned and lived in place.

OLD AGE

Yula Sue Hunting

This old cowboy of mine can't hear half the time.
He has had both eyes skimmed
but still needs glasses to see, and loses them quite
        frequently.

He moseys down to the corral. His hoss is a-calling
        to him.
The old dog a-trotting around friendship eternally
        bound.
He and the old hoss both have kidney troubles.
        Short on air,
the cowboy has an oxygen machine. The old hoss,
        he deals with his naturally.

Now, this old cowboy, when just a kid, consented
        to help fight the big war
overseas. He offered his all for this great country.
Made beachheads on South Pacific Islands. Names
        he had never heard before.
As he left the safety of that old ship with full pack,
        gun and ammo,
he left with a thousand other kids, climbing down
        that old rope ladder.

The landing-barge bucking way up in the air,
       then dropping to nowhere—
Pacific ocean splashing and drenching all out there!
this kid cowboy from dry and arid land.
This sea life not for him and the fear that boils
       within,
those other kids could feel it, too. Fear filled the air.
They finally hit the beach. Blood and death
       everywhere.

Now, these Pacific Isles made pages in history,
       their names
are legendary, going down like Custer's Last Stand,
       Little Big Horn, Geronimo,
Gettysburg or the Battle of the Alamo.

The cowboy has medals to hang on the wall to tell
       of the shots that tattered his
hide and the shrapnel still lodged inside.

This old hoss is crippled, too. His falls and bruises
       all three can attest to.
So, all three bask in yesterday's memories. The
       cowboy has a home and a large
family, but it seems these three share a special
       sentiment and enjoy the time
they are able to share.

Which by the grace of God is only fair.

OLD PETS

Walt McDonald

Hawks in wide, hardscrabble skies track mice
in fields we say we own. We feed too many pets
our children raised by hand and abandoned.
Old bulls aren't worth the hay to save them,

but I don't throw away a glove because it's ugly.
Look at them, old goats and horses fat in the pasture.
That palomino's lame, the oldest mare on the plains,
drools when I rub her ear, can't hear unless I whisper,

leans on me like a post, slobbering oats from my glove,
swishing her tail. This abandoned barn was weeds,
the padlock missing. Thieves hauled good metal off,
nothing but someone's dream holding a roof over stalls,

the cows long slaughtered. Owls watched the plunder
        of doors
in silence. A man with children built this barn
to last, but not one stayed to carry on his herd.
We had to track them down to sign. And now
        the barn is ours,

and pastures fenced by barbed wires dangling
        from posts,
and most of those are broken. We might as well
        breed wolves
or trap for bounty snakes that kill our calves.
We could sell the rattlers' venom for research,

and wolves are bred for national parks in Montana
so why not here? Dawn, I shake my head
    at my schemes
and saddle up, time for rounding strays
and dumping hay to old pets bawling at the barn.

Excerpted from Poetry, Blessings the Body Gave,
published by Ohio State University Press, 1998.

LOSS

Kent Stockton

Lying in my sougans★
With stockdogs nestled close
We kept our vigil from the bathroom floor.
The calf lay in the empty tub,
Still and comatose,
Heedless of the dogs' sporadic snores.

Every hour or so, I checked her—
Tubed her stomach, poured in milk . . .
But never was there any sign of change.
The stutter and the pattern
Of her breathing boded ill,
But the will to keep the life within remained.

The calf was born too early,
In November's coldest dawn,
With snow and frozen clods per Nature's whim.
Too cold, too wet, too early—
And an inattentive mom—
Combined to make this baby's chances grim.

But, oh! The helpless feeling
That hovered in that room
Permeated every move and thought.
The dogs, my faithful stalwarts,
could sense impending doom
And ineffective action come to naught.

The hours passed darkly, slowly,
As her vital functions waned
And the final sigh of life came just at dawn.
Her baby eyes flicked briefly
With her last, unconscious pain—
Kicked once, exhaled, relaxed . . . and she was gone.

The welfare of our livestock
Is a cross we gladly bear,
Though at times the weighty burden takes its toll.
The price we pay for lifestyle
With which none can compare
Is measured not in dollars, but in soul.

*sougans: a cowboy's bedroll

*All across cattle country, when cows are giving birth
during the winter months, orphaned or weakened
calves are brought into the kitchens and bathrooms
of the ranch house. This is done in an effort to warm
the calf, keep a close watch over it, and nurse it back
to health. Usually it works, sometimes it doesn't.*

WE WERE THE HORSEMEN

Andy Wilkinson

We loped across sand hills and stuck to the ridges
to survey the blowouts, then slowed to a trot
to crack through the brush in the cottonwood mottes,
through scrub in the bottoms of each of the washes
where hunkered the wild ones, where rangey ones got

to sidestep the circle our riding was weaving
and stay free, like we felt that we ourselves were
bound only by cowpunching's practical spur
to be in the right place, the right time, and leaving
the rest of the world to kowtow with yes-sir

and no-sir and worry the measured opinion
of people who were not our equals in things
of the land and the sky and all that such brings,
for we were the horsemen and we held dominion
in northern New Mexico, branding in spring.

RITE OF PASSAGE

Jesse Smith

You've been out with the wagon,
Spent your share of time in camp.
You've never been nobody's hero,
Never been some big world champ.

In fact, you're just a cowboy
Out in your part of the West.
You make your livin' horseback,
'Cause that's what you like to do the best.

Some say it's an addiction,
Bad as any booze or dope,
But this addiction revolves around
A horse, a cow, a rope.

Some say, "Oh, how romantic."
Now me, you've got to show
The romanticism in it
When it's zero or below.

And you're a long ways from camp
And you can't feel your toes,
And you've got this great big icicle
Danglin' underneath your nose.

Or when it's hot and dusty
And you can't see or breathe;
The boss man ain't around to quit
And you just can't up and leave.

'Cause you gotta wait till payday
Of that, there's little doubt.
Payday comes, you still can't leave
After they hold your taxes out.

Or when they lead you out a horse
You know it's your bad luck,
And you can see with one eye
This old pony's gonna buck.

But you throw your saddle on him,
Throw caution to the wind.
About the time you slam the ground,
You get your caution back again.

You lay there a-gaspin',
Tryin' hard to catch your breath.
The world around you teeters,
You feel that awful clutch of death.

But you know that you ain't dyin'
When you hear some damned fool say,
As he comes trottin' up,
"Hey, pard, are you okay?"

Or when the rain's a-pourin' down
And your hat dye streaks your face,
And the cattle that you're tryin' to move,
Moves along at a turtle pace.

You think about your cabin
With the stove so nice and warm,
And your horse and cattle turn their heads,
Tryin' not to face the storm.

Or when you got a camp job
And the holidays come 'round,
You know you'll spend them all alone
'Cause you're far from home and town.

You think it's just another day
But when that day begins,
Though you tried hard not to think about it,
Loneliness sets in.

Now you're gettin' old
And your hair's a-turnin gray,
But you think back with fond memories
Of all the yesterdays.

You've never made a fortune,
And you've never gained no fame,
But you've earned the right to have "Cowboy"
Written right beside your name.

Excerpted from Cowboy Poetry: Horse Tracks
Through Sage*, by Sunny Hancock and Jesse Smith,
published by Cowboy Miner Productions.*

FLYING WITH THE EAGLES

Janet Moore

They never were good with money.
Hell, they had nothing to practice on.
Whenever they got a little
They paid bills and then it was gone.

But they knew about cows and grazin'
And how to stretch a dime.
They worked like dogs from dark to dark
Damn near all of the time.

They had a small cow outfit
Bought in their autumn years.
It never reaped a profit,
Just sorrow, stress and tears.

Cattle and land were their only riches.
Memories were their joy.
But years took payment out of them both
In worry 'til health was destroyed.

The bank and drought took over
As loan after loan came due.
Until the rope was at its end
And the money needed didn't come through.

Now . . . they're packin' to leave there.
What little the bank ain't sold
With broken hearts and empty pockets
And memories of purest gold.

Have you ever seen an old, wild cow
Who fought just to stay free?
How she gave up the ghost
When you tied her to that tree?

Sometimes they die right where they stand,
Sometimes after you get 'em home.
But when the freedom is gone
It's over and they don't last long.

Eagles aren't meant for cages.
They need to just fly free
Just like the old, wild cow:
Mom and Dad . . . and me.

SONNET OF THE SAGE

Karen Brown

Wrinkled sky, waves roll by on an April sea,
Streaks of light from foaming white stir the sage,
Showers briefly, ever chiefly, drown me
In grass wild, the Centaur's child. Blessed cage
Of thorny brush that hides in hush the horns
For which we search; a dirt floor church that drives
In narrow sweep, 'tween the steep hidden thorns
Toward winding wheel where waters spill for lives.
Not romantic, but harsh and dry this world
Presents for me hard labor, thirst, and truth.
Upon backs of horn and hide, we built here
Not an easy ride, but bits of sand pearled
From boys to men. We fight by nail and tooth,
We'll keep it rough and save it for the youth.

SKYSAILING

Buck Ramsey (1938–1998)

Oh, God! Hawk am I,
Soaring on a ground sigh
And earth breath.
Shunning all the horsetail wisps,
Searching out the cloudswell lifts,
I skyward press.

Lulling on a lofty plain,
I know that I am not the same
Down from this sky,
Trudging narrow vistaed trails,
Trying to muffle siren wails.
No dread have I,

Nor tones of caution in my talk,
Nor stealth of quarry in my walk,
Nor will to hurt, nor prey to stalk.

*Buck Ramsey wrote this poem in the
early 1970s after a day of soaring above
a friend's New Mexico ranch. This
experience, for a fleeting moment, freed
him from his everyday life spent in a
wheelchair, a condition resulting from
injuries incurred during a "horse wreck"
while Buck was a young working cowboy.*

THE WEIR

Linda Hussa

Tonight I open the ditch through the calf lot.
Ice breaks into puzzle pieces
that will freeze down
never again with this smooth skin.

The calves stand at a distance watching.
Them freshly weaned and curious.
My head down, busy.

When my shovel goes in
the dark ground breaks open
with bright pink water
as the lowering sun lays one thin finger
on my work.

It is quiet. The geese have already bedded
on the lake. The sky is wide and empty
and full.

The calves crowd up behind me
(Red Light, Green Light)
sniffing puffs of sweet oats
on my back, in my hair.

I hear a rustle overhead in the winter branches.
A redtail hawk draws in long wings.
Bare limbs bloom other hawks.
One is white
but rouged with the same sunset
that fills my small ditch.

In memory of Buck Ramsey

"The Weir" will be published in an upcoming collection of
poetry, Tokens in an Indian Graveyard.

MIDNIGHTS ARE MINE

Lyn DeNaeyer Messersmith

Y'know, it's a friendly kind of quiet.
One that ain't, when you study on it some.
Owl's complainin' yonder in the windbreak.
Rations must be scarce; he's soundin' mighty glum.
Guess they's some others that don't sleep so good,
Midnight snackers; tongues scrapin' at the tub.
"Lay still now, got to wash up 'fore you eat,"
That new ma tells a youngster wantin' grub.

Spotlight down the valley. That'll be ol' Jim
Keepin' night guard over on the Rocker T.
Been neighborin' nigh on sixty years or so.
We're no 'count, now, 'cept fer midnights, him an' me.
We've seen a lot of country side by side.
Rode these homesteads many a stormy mile.
Young folk got a different way of thinkin'
But we won't sell our saddles, yet awhile.

Well, hello, youngster, ain't you quite the sight?
Get up there, Gert, let's have a looky-see.
He's a dandy, like them others that you had.
Gonna keep you chasin' in a day or three.
Yer slowin' down like me. This'll be yer last.
Stand steady now. We always understood
One another's way of doin', ain't that so?
Get him dry, ol' gal, you sure do mother good.

I remember when you led 'em all to grass
An' I could hold my own in any test.
But seems we both get easy winded now,
Bringin' up the drag, hopin' fer a rest.
There's days I doubt I even earn my keep.
It's why I volunteer fer midnights now.
Father Time collectin' interest on choices
Made in youth, keeps me wakeful anyhow.

Say, it's right frosty with this window down.
Hill country nights can get that way in spring.
But geese are talkin' over on the pond
An' once I thought I heard a peeper sing.
Moon looks like a mess of silver dollars
Tossed out there on the ripples of the crick.
Reckon if it weren't so gol-durned chilly
I'd linger like some fool that's plumb lovesick.

Well, ol' gal, I guess you got him goin'
So I'll be off to make my midnight rounds,
Checkin' on the rest of yer compadres
Takin' ease out on these star bright beddin' grounds.
So I'll see you sometime after coffee.
I know you'll have him fed an' warmed up fine.
I thank you fer the years that we been pards,
An' you, Lord, that the midnights are still mine.

Excerpted from Ground Tied, *2003*.

WHEN THE CALVES COME

Tom McBeth

Maybe it's genetic or natural selection,
needing to be there when the calves come.
Most everything else seems unimportant,
like growing old, love coming or leaving.
People who can't express themselves
will worry over an old cow or a heifer
like mothers, childless, when the calves come.

When the calves come, along with the laughing,
spanking new, beckoning, Spring, green grass
yearning softly sighs like earth's breath,
pleading with wisps of wind, like spirits.
The grass, from natural selection, has roots
like arteries, intertwined in their hearts.

Spring or the heart or the spirit will not
be complete without the natural selection,
those, who yearn to be among
whispering or thunder-welting winds,
sighing or screaming through the new grass.
Since our time began there are some who
will never rest when the calves come.

CHAPTER 4

FAMILY
& THE
COMMUNITY
OF
COWBOYS

Family is where you find it. Sometimes family is not joined by blood and genetics but by a common lifestyle or the needed friendship of your closest neighbor. Among the poems in this chapter, we see a saddle-bronc rider paying homage to a revered champion; a cantankerous grandfather who prods everyone out of bed in the mornings; an uncle scattering the ashes of an old cowboy friend; a father chronicling a musical heritage that was passed from his own mother to his son; and a son learning the hard lessons of life while working with a cowboy crew.

JERRY AMBLER

Paul Zarzyski

JERRY AMBLER

Your marker with its bucking horse twister
carved in marble, with gold-buckle words
World Champion Saddle Bronc Rider 1946
facing Blue Mountain outside Monticello, Utah,
would move anyone who's ever craved
with every gritty molecule of his makeup
a winning spur ride—cocked his hammer,
nodded for the gate, marked one rocketing out,
fought for holts and felt every 1,300-pound
ounce of quick and hard and sinewy
swordfish ballerina between his knees.

JERRY AMBLER

You don't know me from Adam's off-ox
and even if you could, times these days change
too drastically to say maybe we'd have driven
the same Cadillacs or Hudsons between pitchin's,
savored the same label of rye chased with dames
you'd no doubt be unspooling your bedroll beside
before I could even reach my *how-do-ma'am*
John B. hat brim—handsome, tan, lanky,
grinning booger that you were in *Life*
and *Look* magazine Chesterfield cigarette ads.

You bet, only a damn fool palavers to the dead,
but I savvy, here and now, how the West
I've come to love bucks-on in the wild
blood passing through some porous sandrock
canyon wall of time between your ride and mine.
I feel its *rounder* pulse still pounding
behind Powder River bucking chutes. I hear—
decades past my rodeo prime as I slip
this shiny fifty-cent piece into the slot
between marble and earth—Ian Tyson
resurrecting your story in a ranahan rap
forking beauty with truth, the old sittin' new,
solid as gospel in the roughstock middle.

KITCHEN WINDOW COWBOY

Jan Swan Wood

From the kitchen's west window I gaze outside,
And see the saddle horses that I seldom get to ride.
Slick hair glistens over muscle and fat.
No sweat marks the long winter hair on their backs.

I've watched the ranch seasons pass on this place,
With cold window glass pressed hard to my face.
And longed for the wind to be there instead.
Longed for the work on which my soul has fed.

For most of my life, I've been out in the sun,
Working a-horseback to get a job done.
Smelling the dust, the mud or the snow.
Feeling blistering heat or winter's cold blow.

But the seasons don't change much where I spend
    my days now.
The housework and such keeps me busy, and how.
Then I look out and see the night horse lift his head.
Dishes can wait, I must see what he sees instead.

Out the south windows, I watch the cows coming in,
And the riders who push them to the corrals
    once again.
Dust billows up and they bawl and they mill,
Then in spite of their dragging, through the big gate
    they spill.

I've changed windows twice to take it all in,
Now I'm perched by the north one so I won't miss
    a thing.
But it's just not the same as being out there.
I don't get dusty or smell the cow in the air.

I've watched the cows calve and seen the calves get
    a brand.
Seen them sorted and weaned as by the window
    I stand.
I smell the smoke and the dust, the vaccine and more,
But it's on my man's clothes when he comes
    through the door.

My heart aches with longing for the times in the past,
When my cow work was done horseback and not
    through the glass
Of windows that separate me from the days
Of cowboying for a living and not just for pay.

Then a small sound behind me brings my gaze
    back inside
To the reason I don't get to cowboy and ride.
A sweet baby boy has awoke from his nap,
And crawls over to me and wants up on my lap.

Then we gaze out together at the cow work below.
I hug him up close and right then I know
That what I gave up is small and I wouldn't trade it,
    by heck,
For this little boy hugging me tight 'round the neck.

It won't be too long 'til he'll be alongside
Of his daddy and me as we set out to ride.
So I'll be a kitchen window cowboy, and now
     I s'pose you understand.
They're only babies once and I'll enjoy him
     while I can.

THIRD SADDLING

B. Lynne McCarthy

August winds crossing Dad's
Old pole horse pens
Carried the quiet timbre of
His words, "If I were you . . ."

Wisdom from a figure solid
As the native cedar post
He's shaded up under.
Watching, gently advising,
While a green colt and green kid
Work through the kinks.

But on the third day he
Opened the corral gate.
The colt and I were turned
Loose, free to go on our own.

Maybe those hot afternoons
Weren't so much about
Breaking colts
As a father preparing
A daughter for life.

LOVE IS BLIND

Doris Daley

Meet Jake, my darling sweetheart. Oh, I know he's
    got his flaws.
But I think I'm hearing wedding bells and I'm
    trapped in love's steel jaws.
Oh, I know he's kind of lazy, and not particular bright.
I'll admit that even from afar he's not a pretty sight.

His nose is rather purplish, while the hair in his ears
    is black,
And his eyeballs are so cross-eyed that the tears run
    down his back.
What teeth he has are yellow and he long ago lost
    all his hair.
Why, to look at his head is like heaven for there is
    no parting there.

I know you could never accuse him of being a
    learned man.
If brains were lard, Jake ain't got enough to grease a
    frying pan.
But he is a good conversationalist, could regale you
    for hours and hours,
Just as long as it's one of three topics: drought,
    mules or scours.

But here's a plus, he's frugal. He gets that from his
   mother's side.
Now there's a woman who'd skin a fly to get the
   tallow and hide.
She'd drive you to your own funeral and then
   charge you for the ride,
And her pancakes are so pitifully thin they only
   have one side.

Folks have warned me he's belligerent and likes to
   pick a fight—
But, only when he's sober, so I'm probably alright.
He's a man who loves his shut-eye and to hear him
   snore ain't pretty;
If napping were an Olympic event he'd have been
   at Salt Lake City.

I can't fix his chronic gas pains and I know he's
   immature.
And as for the halitosis, the doc says there's no cure.
I'm not blind to his shortcomings; I know love
   extracts a price.
But carbolic soap can cure a lot and he's only been
   jailed twice!

Oh, my heart is all a-flutter. He's the man I vowed
   I'd wait for—
'Cause Jake's a man with a real good well and his
   ranch and cows are paid for!

HOLLYHOCKS

Audrey Hankins

Hollyhocks and old ranch wives
Both thrive on so little care,
Bringing beauty to barren places,
Enduring year after year.

They're at it again, the old men,
Reliving their glory days;
Cattle they caught, horses they made,
Cowboy pride, cowboy ways.

An old wife moves among them,
Invisible but for coffee pot.
They don't see her leave, or care that she goes
To smile and tend her hollyhocks.

She shares no glory stories,
Her choice was a supporting role.
Freeing her man to follow his call,
She felt privileged just to fill a hole.

She was the one left holding the gather,★
For hours she'd highpoint alone,
'Til she often wondered if they'd changed the plan,
Forgotten her and gone on home.

Relegated to ride drag★ with the little kids,
She ate dust while planning meals.
No good hand could be spared for that,
He wouldn't remember how it feels.

She did up the jobs left undone
By men with better things to do—
Doctored horses, milked the cow,
Ran the kids to school.

She brushed the backs of her bucket dogies,★
The way mother cows lick their calves,
'Til they glowed and gained on her tender care.
She never nurtured by halves.

Now her waist is thick, her hair is thin,
And her knees are stiff when she walks,
A solitary figure out in the yard,
Humming and tending her hollyhocks.

Hollyhocks and old ranch wives
Both thrive on so little care,
Bringing beauty to barren places,
Enduring year after year.

★*holding the gather:* on horseback, containing a herd
of cattle rounded up, or gathered

★*ride drag:* on horseback, riding behind a moving
herd of cattle, an often slow, tedious and dusty job

★*bucket dogies:* orphan calves fed with a bucket. This
chore is usually done by the ranch wife, whose
mothering skills give her an added advantage.

TRADITIONS

Sandy Seaton

The smell of the land, the feel in your hand
Brings ranchin' home to me.
The bawl of a calf, the hired hand's laugh,
The new grass I can see.

Risin' at dawn with a stretch and a yawn,
Watchin' the land grow light;
The cows head to drink and I start to think
On things that just ain't right.

I'm a newcomer here; I bought my first steer
When I was just seventeen.
But some fellers now, they all owned their cows
Before they were rightly weaned.

Families had cattle—born to the saddle,
Tied to the land by birth.
Their folks built the brand; the old ones had sand,
The ranch proved their life and worth.

But Charlie just called; he had a bad fall—
Another year of drought.
Sold his calves low, the bankers say no,
Auction man will be out.

Ol' Rusty's in town, a yard small and brown,
Down at the mill, loadin' feed.
His kids runnin' wild, left Irene for that child,
Hayfields all gone to seed.

It surely was sad when Joe got hurt bad.
Cowboy and hand in his day.
He had to sell out, his boys left no doubt
The city's where they would stay.

Corporations moved in—don't understand kin—
Just countin' profit and loss.
Billy could stay but he went on his way,
Used to his dad bein' boss.

This mornin' I'm wakin' to old ways a-breakin'.
So many are goin' down.
Lord, give families the grace to hang onto their
     place
And keep them out of town.

Excerpted from The Yellowstone Poet, *published by*
Hound Dog Press.

DADDY'S BELLS

Colen Sweeten

My daddy was a freighter,
His wagons rolled across the West,
With Daddy in the driver's seat,
A silver chain across his vest.
He built a cabin on a homestead
In the edge of friendly pines,
But the only way to save the ranch
Was haulin' freight up to the mines.
I helped Mother run the ranch
The best that we knew how;
Daddy took most all the horses
But we always had a cow.

Sometimes I'd step outside the house
At night when it was late,
I'd walk down the lane to meet him
And just stand there by the gate.
The stars above would glisten
Where the road winds through the hills,
I'd hold my breath and listen
For the sound of Daddy's bells.
At last when he came rollin' in
From that long and dusty ride,
He'd step down and hand the reins to me
And hug my mother till she cried.

*Colen explains this poem: "The early wagon freighters
had a short string of bells hanging on the harness of the
lead team. On mountain roads or at night, the driver
would stop the team at one of the wide spots in the road,
called 'turnouts,' and rest his horses while he listened for
the sound of other freighters' bells. If he could hear bells,
he would wait until the other wagon had passed so they
wouldn't have trouble trying to pass on a narrow road."*

RODE MY SON'S HORSE
THIS MORNIN'

Gary Robertson

I rode my son's horse this mornin'
With Daddy's Capriola kack.*
I strapped on Grandad's workin' spurs
Just ta kinda bring 'em back.

See, Grandad's gone now fifteen years,
An' Daddy's moved to town.
Last week my boy went off to school.
Guess I just got ta feelin' down.

Oh, I know Grandad's in a better place
An' Daddy's surely earned his rest.
My boy, he's got his life to lead,
An' I know it's for the best.

It just don't seem that long ago
We all worked here side by side—
Four generations sharin' daily chores
History an' pride.

But that was then, an' this is now.
I start each day out all alone—
An', no, it ain't the work that bothers me,
It's the workin' all alone.

No, I ain't the first to feel like this;
Just my turn, I guess you'd say.
Ya know, I never saw it comin',
Never dreamed I'd feel this way.

Lord, Grandad must-a felt this way
In nineteen-forty-one
When he sent a soldier off to war,
His one and only son.

An' Daddy must-a felt like this
When I chose to hit the road,
When I went to chasin' rodeo
An' he stayed to tote the load.

So, now I guess it's my turn
To do what needs be done—
An' I'll do it for my grandad,
My daddy an' my son

An' every now an' then I'll ease the pain
That lonesome sometimes brings
by usin' their old chaps an' ropes
An' kacks an' piggin' strings.★

An' I'll ride my son's horse some mornin's
With Daddy's Capriola kack,
An' I'll strap on Grandad's workin' spurs
An' be glad to bring 'em back.

★*Capriola kack:* The Capriola saddle shop in Elko, Nevada,
is widely known for their finely made working saddles.
"Kack" is a buckaroo term for a saddle and rigging.

★*piggin' strings:* short pieces of rope or lariat used to tie a
calf's feet together after he's been thrown to the ground,
thus keeping him from getting up while the cowboy
doctors him

ODE TO MY LADY, MY WIFE

Sunny Hancock (1931–2003)

I had all my Christmas shopping done,
all that I had to do,
All that I had left to get this year
was one small gift for you;

The sort of thing I find
with which is very simply dealt,
A gift which would explain to you
exactly how I felt.

Then my mind began to wander,
as my mind will sometimes do,
Running back along the days and times
and years I've spent with you.

And as I got to thinking
of those cherished yesterdays,
It dawned on me that we've been
down the road quite a ways.

We've worked some tacky ranches
and we lived in weathered shacks,
Where the wind would blow the lamp out
when it whistled through the cracks.

You'd take care of me and both the kids,
and hold a job in town,
And still have time to smile
and spread a lot of love around.

If I'd come home disgusted,
grumbling 'bout the job I had,
Just a little time with you
and then things wouldn't look so bad.

Then later when we'd bought the ranch
and you cooked at the school,
I was workin' in the woods
all day, so, usually, as a rule

You'd have to do the feedin',
chop the ice and, if you could,
Milk the cow and feed the "leppies"★
and then sometimes split some wood.

And I'd get home way after dark
from puttin' in my hours;
I'd find that you'd just pulled a calf
or maybe doctored one with scours.★

You never did complain much,
always had a lot of heart;
Only maybe just to mention
that the tractor wouldn't start.

Then when school was out for summer,
golly, what a happy day.
You could spend it changing handline,★
floodin', workin' in the hay.

Should have had three men
to help with all the work you had to do.
I'd be there afternoons and weekends
and somehow we made it through.

And now when you look in the mirror
at the lady standing there,
Why, there's some wrinkles in her forehead,
and some silver in her hair.

She's maybe packin'
just a little bit of extra weight,
And you don't like what you see there,
but to me, she sure looks great.

So while we're lookin' at that image,
why, we maybe won't agree,
But here's what that reflection
standin' up there means to me:

She's my Wife and she's my Partner,
she's my Mate and she's my Friend,
She's the Mother of my children,
she's my Lover, then again,

My Companion on life's highway;
she'll light up the blackest night.
Life seems just a wee bit better
any time that she's in sight.

She's my Teacher, an she's taught me
that life really can be fun.
Don't you worry 'bout a few gray hairs,
you've earned 'em, every one.

Now as far as Christmas shoppin',
guess I didn't do so good,
Bought you something pretty common
like you might have known I would.

Since your present ain't so special
and it ain't too big a deal,
I thought I'd write a note to you
and tell you kinda how I feel.

If God would grant a wish for me
(I'm sure just one would do),
I'd simply wish that I could spend
a lot more years with you.

Your Loving Husband

leppies: orphaned calves, dogies

scours: diarrhea in calves

handline: long pieces of irrigation pipe
   that must be moved each day

floodin': flood irrigation

Excerpted from Cowboy Poetry: Horse Tracks
Through Sage, *by Sunny Hancock and Jesse Smith,
published by Cowboy Miner Productions.*

A SCATTERING OF ASHES

Vess Quinlan

The old cowboy left instructions
on how and where
his remains were to be placed.
"Along the ridge," he said,
"and out across the little meadow
where the elk come first in spring."

It would be a hard climb to where
the old man wanted to spend eternity.
A good chance, my uncle thought,
to school a big broncy colt
He'd started on that fall.
Hard work should tire the youngster,
maybe damp his fire a bit,
so he could learn the skills my uncle taught.

The big roan behaved
as though he understood
the solemn mission they were on
and lulled my uncle careless
of the popping sound a stopper
makes when pulled from urn.
The horse showed a definite
lack of respect for cowboy funerals,
And threw a bucking, squalling, fit.

By the time my uncle got the fool's head up
and whacked him good with the urn,
the old man's ashes were gone.
What hadn't been inhaled or dissolved
in horse sweat were stomped into the ridge.

My uncle swears that above his cussing,
gagging, spitting out of ashes
and the snorts of the silly roan colt,
He could hear his old friend laughing.

*Vess explains: "The story this poem came from
happened on Hatchet Cattle Company's Mountain
Meadows Ranch sometime in the late '30s or early
'40s. The old man was a WWI combat veteran who
had, I suppose, seen enough of people and felt safer
on an isolated ranch with horses, dogs and cattle. He
and a few other old bachelor cowboys I actually knew
would hire on a ranch fresh home from the war and
stay there until they died. If the ranch sold, they went
with the place just like the corrals and cattle guards."*

LESSONS

Dan Schmitt

One thousand seven games of rummy
    were played beneath the shade
Of our modern-day chuckwagon,
    a broke-down trailer truck.
So skillfully each hand was dealt,
    so cautious was it played,
The winner voiced his victory
    and the losers cursed bad luck.

Then later, after supper,
    our evening hours were lost
Shoeing horses, roping bushes
    and reading western books,
Taking turns at telling stories,
    taking rough looks from the boss
And hearing the foul-mouthed repertoire
    from the kitchen of the cook.

It would seem a lovely evening,
    filled with cowboy merriment,
But enjoyment from this ritual
    was not what we derived.
See, none of us wanted to be there,
    rather in our tents,
But we had to wait till sundown
    or in there we'd broil alive.

On the outside acting saddened,
        but smiling from within,
We'd amble to our teepees when
        the temperature was right.
Dog-tired, muscles aching
        from the day's ten-hour ride,
We'd burn the ticks out of our legs
        and drift off for the night.

The slam of an egg-filled frying pan
        would wake us from near death,
The wrangler would unsaddle,
        we'd stumble to the shack
To scarf our food like animals,
        no time to take a breath,
Then out to catch the horses
        and race to cinch your kack.★

Camp coffee gets cold fast
        when it's drunk at three A.M.
It gets down in your stomach
        and it starts to turn to ice.
You feel as though it will surely
        come creeping up again,
And you may complain about it once,
        but you'll never do it twice.

'Cause sniveling isn't something
        taken kindly by this lot.
You're apt to get a razzin' that could
        last you near a week.
You grit your teeth and bear it,
        thank God for what you got,
Remembering that predators wait
        to feed upon the meek.

The temperature hits ninety,
    my throat gets hot and dry.
Cows are getting squirrelly,
    hard to keep them all in line.
Jim looks back across the valley,
    sees the one that I passed by,
And begins to get "that look"
    as prickles move up my spine.

No one but me could understand
    the reason for his words.
If I told you what he said,
    your impression would be wrong.
They were like sharpened daggers
    and as vicious as I've heard,
But they were laced with good intentions
    and I knew it all along.

Still, they were so hard to handle
    as they cut down to the core.
He'd get right down to yellin';
    he could go on for a mile.
I never expected favors;
    hard work and nothing more.
Sometimes, though, I wished like heck
    that just once he'd crack a smile.

The boys are getting moody,
    we go through this every day.
They need someone to blame it on
    and I'm the greenhorn kid
Pat always had a mean streak
    that came out in strange ways,
And we couldn't please him either,
    no matter what we did.

Still, somehow we always managed
    to try to work together,
Though I must admit at times
    murder may have crossed my mind.
When the work was done that evening,
    things would all get better;
We'd sit there in the shade
    and play rummy to unwind.

See, it's just another day,
    nothing special, nothing new.
It would be the same
    on any ranch, I think.
I just tried to keep on doing
    all the things I had to do,
And reached up for a firm hold
    so I wouldn't start to sink.

Now, gazing through the heat waves
    that slither through the air,
I can see a yellow pickup kicking dust
    and riding high.
It's time that I got back for school,
    and I never thought I'd care,
But looking through that rearview mirror,
    I feel like I could cry.

'Cause it isn't what you couldn't do
    or what you didn't know
That really makes a difference
    when it all comes to an end.
It's how hard you tried while you were failing
    and the lessons that helped you grow
That make you look back one hellish summer
    and wish you were there again.

kack: a buckaroo term for a saddle and rigging

124

THE LAST FIDDLER
AT FRENCHMAN'S

Paul Schmitt

Papa got it from a drunkard
Who had squandered all his money
And the fiddle was the last thing
That he had of any worth.
So, bartered for a bottle,
It became her prized possession.
A fiddle's what she wanted
More than anything on earth.

Finished blonde rather than walnut,
No one'd seen one just quite like it.
An angel pictured on the back
And a tone so rich and true.
As she rode west in the wagon
She would practice by the hour
A little tune she'd worked out,
The only one she knew.

She sawed upon that fiddle
All the way across the prairie
'Til everyone but Papa
Wished they'd left it in St. Joe.
They all said, "Girl, if you don't
Learn a new one, we'll go crazy,
And that darn tune 'Boil the Cabbage'
Will be the only one you know."

The wagon master said that
The "pony rider" told him
Of a new place, Frenchman's Station,
They could rest a day or more.
They stopped, not realizing
That the place the Frenchman built there
Would stand more than a century
And never close its door.

Other wagons stopped there,
And with a brand new audience
The first fiddler at Frenchman's
Played from early in the day,
'Til one by one the listeners
Found other chores and pastimes,
'Cause the tune called "Boil the Cabbage"
Was all that she could play.

Many years and many wagons,
Many cowboys from the ranches,
All would gather at the Frenchman's
And the music would abound
From the fiddles and the guitars,
The jew's harps and the banjos.
The Saturday night dances
Would bring folks from miles around.

We were driving east from Fallon,
Headed out to Monitor Valley
But anticipating milkshakes
Often times enjoyed before.
Thick and rich, each favorite flavor
Ordered without hesitation,
For we'd never passed it by—
Frenchman's Bar, Cafe and Store.

We topped the pass and looked down
To the flats of Dixie Valley
To the place where we intended
To make our usual stop.
There was nothing but a bare spot—
The lone tree already dying,
They'd made a grave for all that history
And spread gravel on the top.

Saddened, still we stopped there,
Took some drinks out of the cooler,
Toasted all the travelers
Who had stopped through time of yore.
Felt sorry for the people
Who would speed by never knowing
That once there was a place there—
Frenchman's Bar, Cafe and Store.

As he would often do when
He was just a-learning,
Dan took out the fiddle
His grandma'd held so dear.
I broke out my guitar,
We leaned against the pickup,
Played a tune for the dying cottonwood
And a leaf fell like a tear.

His fiddle's blonde rather than walnut,
No one's seen one just quite like it.
And angel pictured on the back,
An heirloom from the pioneer day.
And the last fiddler at Frenchman's
Played a little tune he'd worked out—
A tune called "Boil the Cabbage,"
The only one that he could play.

CHAPTER 5

LOOKIN' BACK DOWN THE TRAIL

The contemporary cowboy life is closely linked with its historical counterpart. In many ways, the work today is done the same as it was at the turn of the last century. Yes, there are innovations in equipment and utilization of trucks, horse trailers and even four-wheelers at times. But the feelings of isolation, dependence upon family members, and dealing with the forces of nature remain the same. Therefore, it comes naturally for a cowboy poet to look back down the trail, from "whence he came."

BEHOLD A PALE HORSE

Mike Logan

And I looked, and behold a pale horse:
and his name that sat on him was Death,
and Hell followed with him.

—Revelation 6:8

Montana 1886.
A pale horse first appears
White shadow on a drought–struck range,
The coldest fall in years.

That horse he first was sighted
Up north on Crooked Creek
The day the year's worst storm blew in
And howled for more'n a week.

He seemed some awful phantom,
Some harbinger of doom,
That pale horse lopin' cold and gaunt
Through winter's gatherin' gloom.

Most outfits wintered cows that year
That usu'lly they'd a-sold,
'Cause cattle prices dropped so far
That cowmen chanced the cold.

He ghosted down the Musselshell
Behind a warm chinook,
Froze sheaths of ice on all the grass
With just his pale-eyed look.

That horse loped towards the Judith
And filled that range with dread,
'Cause where he went great blizzards struck
And whole cow herds lay dead.

He worked his evil 'cross the plains
And up the Little Dry,
Wreaked havoc as he passed that way.
More herds laid down to die.

It got to where to cut his track
Filled cowmen's hearts with fear
As coulees★ clogged with starvin' cows
That grim and direful year.

Cowhands lost toes and fingers
As they fought to save their herds.
The sight of cattle dyin' slow
Was pain too fierce for words.

That horse's passin' iced the streams
And thirst-crazed steers broke through
And drowned as others pushed 'em in.
Weren't nothin' man could do.

When spring, it finally came that year,
Old–timers still take vows
That men could walk for miles and miles
On carcasses of cows.

The hell that followed with that horse
Was in the eyes of men
Who'd rolled the dice with nature
And seen their life's dreams end.

They called it The Hard Winter.
It blew the winds of change
When Death, he rode a pale horse
And killed the open range.

coulees: small dry streambeds

Excerpted from Laugh Kills Lonesome and
Other Poems, *published by Buglin' Bull Press.*

TO AN OLD FRIEND

Red Steagall

I stood by the fountain as they brought him out,
A lost, lonely look on his face.
I ain't never seen him in nothin' but boots.
The wheelchair shore seemed out of place.

It took him awhile to recall who I am,
But confusion turned into a grin.
It was though we were saddled up, ready to ride
The Hackberry pasture again.

He laughed as he said, "I remember the time
That yeller bronc swallered his head,
And pitched you so high that you turned over twice.
Me'n Benny Bob swore you was dead."

He looked up at me and asked, "How is old Ben?"
I lied and said, "He's doin' fine."
No need to remind him his brother was gone.
Ben died back in seventy nine.

For most of an hour we rode at a trot.
We branded and shaped up the steers,
Drank gallons of coffee, ate sourdough bread,
And cowboyed for 51 years.

I thought he's an old man when I was a kid,
At a time when I needed a friend,
He took me to raise, taught me all that I know,
'Bout horses and cattle and men.

My daddy had died and I needed a job.
I's big for a kid of fifteen.
They put me to work on the Four 6's Ranch.
Was dumb as a gourd and as green.

We's lookin' for strays in the Wichita Breaks—
Me and John Gaither and him,
I lost sight of John so I's lookin' around,
A daydreamin' there on the rim.

Rode up on some cattle hid out in the brush,
A two-year-old steer come by me,
Throwed a nine in his tail and cut a new trail
Right out through some salt cedar trees.

I took in behind him a givin' it hell.
The colt I was ridin' was green.
I thought to myself, he ain't gettin' away—
This roan is a runnin' machine.

Was goin' full bore when we got to the bank,
The stream wasn't wide as my hat.
I nearly pulled up, but I thought, What the hell—
I've jumped rivers wider than that.

I bogged that old pony plumb up to his gut,
Was wallerin' and thrashin' around;
He's goin' down deeper with each desperate lunge,
Me prayin' he'd find solid ground.

Just at the moment that I heard his voice,
A rope appeared right by the roan
"Get outa that kack and hang onto my line!
The colt'll get out on his own."

I've crossed that old river many a time;
I've found me a bog once or twice.
But I still remember a thirty-foot rope
And a good cowboy piece of advice:

"When you ride the river, son, make sure your horse
Is gentle and seasoned as well,
'Cause only the gooduns will get you across.
That quicksand goes clean down to hell."

I got up to leave and he reached for my hand,
Said, "Son, I'm sure glad you dropped by.
If you see old Ben, have him saddle my horse:
I hate sittin' waitin' to die."

His voice started crackin', he swallered and said,
"I'm nearin' the end of my ride.
If I cross the river before you get there,
I'll leave a good horse on this side."

Excerpted from Ride for the Brand, *published by*
Bunkhouse Press.

SONGS ON THE NIGHTWIND

Virginia Bennett

Pennies saved on a rough-cut shelf,
  safely hidden in a Log Cabin tin,
behind a Clabber Girl can, it seemed a sweet place
  to be banking daydreams in.

She was the bride of a prairie pioneer,
  building her home from a shanty of sod.
And each day, she labored 'til she was all used up,
  and only inwardly questioned her God.

Each day, seeing no one but her husband,
  no solace could her wounded heart find.
Grubbing out sagebrush, she even led a blind mule,
  while her man, bless his heart, trudged behind.

Harder than the mule did the homesteader work.
  He chased daylight from dawn 'til dark.
Nighttime would find him exhausted and spent,
  with no strength for laughter or lark.

"You work, you survive. You don't, you die,"
  was the homesteader's philosophy of life.
Too busy surviving, he couldn't perceive
  the tender yearnings of his prairie wife.

So, she pored over the ragged, worn pages
  of a Sears Roebuck Consumer's Guide.
Yet, only one item enticed her spirit
  and caused her to light up inside.

It was a canary she dreamed of,
  in a dandy, brass-wired cage.
A canary who'd sing softly, yet listen
  to all her pent-up longings and rage.

So, she squirreled away her savings
  from the sale of her Barred Rock hens' eggs,
and she sneaked in her secret Sears order
  right after liniment for her husband's sore legs.

On the day the mysterious order arrived,
  her husband's wrath openly vented.
For he hated (or feared) her defiant act,
  and the freedom the bird represented.

But the bird, blessed with ignorance,
  sang and trilled, bringing the sod shack back to life.
And each evening, in rosy glow of kerosene lamp,
  a smile graced the face of the wife.

Until the day that she ran to the cabin,
  astonished at there what she'd find.
The door stood ajar, the cage door, as well.
  Done either by accident or design.

Days later, she found her canary.
  He lay under a tree, stone dead.
And she cried no tears as she carried him home,
  for they would have been bitter tears shed.

She wrapped him a white linen hanky,
  embroidered, the way wives sometimes do.
And she kept him to remember that sad day,
  when out the door, her heart's melody flew.

Excerpted from Canyon of the Forgotten,
self-published.

THE OLD PROSPECTOR

Jack Hannah

Well, he headed out the canyon
    one late autumn in the snow.
The old prospector with his mule
    was loaded, movin' slow.
He'd buttoned high his collar
    with his hat stuck down like glue.
And he headed straight for Elko 'cause—
    he'd always wanted to.

Well, he chewed a twist of somethin'
    that would most surely curl your hair.
His long beard matched his steel-gray eyes
    with their penetratin' stare.
He moved with calm demeanor.
    He seemed fearless through an' through.
And he headed straight for Elko 'cause—
    he'd always wanted to.

Well, his mule was short and wiry,
    and his face was long and sad.
He had a way a' goin'
    much like his owner had.
They seemed to go together,
    and both to each was true.
And they headed straight for Elko 'cause—
    they'd always wanted to.

As they hoofed it into Elko
    all the cowboys crowded 'round.
They'd just come off the gather
    and was shootin' up the town.
They spied the old prospector
    and decided what they'd do.
And for fun, they bunched up around 'im 'cause—
    they'd always wanted to.

One asked the old prospector,
    "Have you ever learned to dance?"
He said, "No (in a shy way).
    You see, I ain't never had the chance."
Well, the cowboy pulled his six-gun an' said,
    "Well, I'm up to teachin' you."
And he danced that night in Elko
    just as if he'd wanted to.

Well, he danced around those bullets there
    just like a jumpin' jack.
He counted six, an' ceased to dance,
    an' stepped swiftly to his pack.
He held a shotgun in his hands,
    and his voice came soft and cool.
He said, "Sonny, tell me, sonny,
    have you ever kissed a mule?"

The young lad's face contorted
    as he pondered his disgrace.
As he stared with consternation
    at the shotgun in his face.
He tried to speak, and swallered hard,
    as his voice came softly through.
He said, "No, I've never kissed a mule—
    but I've always wanted to!"

HOW FAR IS LONESOME

Yvonne Hollenbeck

My mama got a letter from Aunt Jessie yesterday
and she said that it is lonesome where she's at;
you know, I really miss her since she up and
    moved away;
Mama showed me where she went on our old map.

Aunt Jessie married Hiram and he took her far
    from me
and it really made me sad she moved away,
'cause she told me I was special and she played with
    me a lot,
but I told her I'd come visit her someday.

I can ride my little pony and I'll take along my doll
so I won't have to make the trip alone.
We will go and visit Jessie and I know that she
    won't care
if we spend a week or two in her new home.

Mama said she's on a homestead, whatever that
    might be,
and Jessie don't have neighbors where she lives.
Hiram's busy working, so she spends her days alone
and she always seemed to like us little kids.

So, if you'll kindly tell me just how far 'way
    Lonesome is
I will saddle up and head there yet today;
I'll be riding off to Lonesome where my dear Aunt
    Jessie is
and I sure hope Lonesome isn't far away.

Excerpted from Where Prairie Flowers Bloom and
other poems, *self-published, 2002.*

THE RIDER THAT NEVER MADE GOOD

Rhoda Sivell (1874–1962)

You look at the men that are lucky,
　You tell me they're fated to be,
You say that they got all the chances;
　There's none left for you or for me.
That's why we grope in the darkness,
　That's why we stumble and fall;
But I tell you the Great God above us
　Has given such chances to all.

Have you wasted the years of your manhood?
　Have you squandered the days of your youth?
And now you are talking of chances,
　And we know you're not telling the truth.
Have you idled when other men labored?
　Yes, they toiled when the sun set low;
By the sweat of their brow they've "made good,"
　And you tell us 'twas luck made them so.

Have you stood in the storm at its fiercest?
　Not a foot of the way could you make;
But you're holding your cattle from drifting,
　Yes, these are the chances you take.
With the snow hissing past like a rattler,
　And the prairie a whirling, white hell,
And you're freezing, and cussing, and praying,
　But the bunch they are standing it well.

And when you get back to the ranch house,
    You swear you'll do it no more;
But the next storm that hits the prairie,
    You'll be out where you were before.
For a man is a man at all times,
    And in trouble a man's at his best;
For when adversity hits him
    It puts his strength to the test.

Did you ride to your horses at midnight,
    When the world all lay asleep,
And the wolves they were running the yearlings
    Away in the coulees★ deep?
Did you go in the night to guard them,
    For you tell me you lost them so?
I guess you slept on in the bunk-house,
    And just let the yearlings go.

And now you're talking of chances;
    But we haven't time to wait
To listen to lame excuses
    Of the man who is up against fate.
For a man is a man at all times,
    And I know that we like him best
When he's fighting the storm at its fiercest,
    And putting his strength to the test.

★*coulees:* small dry streambeds

Excerpted from Voices from the Range, *1912.*

THE MEN THAT DON'T FIT IN

Robert W. Service (1874–1958)

There's a race of men that don't fit in,
  A race that can't stay still;
So they break the hearts of kith and kin,
  And they roam the world at will.
They range the field and they rove the flood
  And they climb the mountain's crest.
Theirs is the curse of the gypsy blood,
  And they don't know how to rest.

If they just went straight, they might go far,
  They are strong and brave and true;
But they're always tired of the things that are,
  And they want the strange and new.
They say: "Could I find my proper groove,
  What a deep mark I would make!"
So they chop and change, and each fresh move
  Is only a fresh mistake.

And each forgets, as he strips and runs
  With a brilliant, fitful pace,
It's the steady, quiet, plodding ones
  Who win in the lifelong race.
And each forgets that his youth has fled,
  Forgets that his prime is past,
Till he stands one day, with a hope that's dead,
  In the glare of the truth at last.

He has failed, he has failed;
   he has missed his chance;
  He has just done things by half.
Life's been a jolly joke on him,
  And now is the time to laugh.
Ha, ha! He is one of the Legion Lost;
  He was never meant to win.
He's a rolling stone, and it's bred in the bone;
  He's a man who won't fit in.

MEMORIES

Ross Knox

You sit in your chair and you stare at the wall
And you relive the days when you rode proud and tall
While making the big drives, rope and brand
And just practice the art of making a hand.
You was just a kid when you left your home
and headed north to the Yellowstone
to those high mountain meadows in a pristine land
that's yet to be ruined by human hand
and it still brings a smile when you relive the ride
on a moonlit night across the great divide
with the northern lights sparkling like diamonds
    and jewels,
just you and God and a string of mules.
You made your camp up on Two Ocean Creek
and you let the sound of the water sing you to sleep.
And those high desert ranches on the Nevada range
where for the last hundred years there's been darned
    little change.
At night, 'round the chuck wagon, you wished folks
    could see
that you and the mustang, the only thing left that's free.
From a hilltop you'd stare at the vast expanse . . .
it seemed you could trot forever and hit no fence.
With no time clock or desk, each day we'd thank God
that we're not a slave to the urban mob.

Yes, you'd chosen to ride a trail seldom traveled,
little knowing how fast it can all come unraveled.
Remember the winter of '73?
It was the beginning of the end for men like me.
You were on top of the world, and then overnight
the cow market dropped clear out of sight.
It just kept getting worse with each passing day
till a cow wasn't hardly worth giving away.
You'd spent your whole life keeping a tradition alive,
now each day's a constant battle to just try and survive.
But, though the cost of grass keeps going up and
        cow prices keep falling,
being a cowboy is still the highest calling.
Now, you're a prisoner to a chair that has wheels,
but you still remember the way that it feels
to step across a good horse, and a custom-made saddle
and the thrill of running mustangs, and tying down
        wild cattle.
For the last forty years you've had the same loving wife
and there's not much you'd change about your life,
But when the memories come calling you can't help
        but pray:
Lord, please make me a cowboy again for a day.

HALLIE LONNIGAN

Tom Russell

My name is Hallie Lonnigan
I married Walter Jones
"For better or for worse," so said
The Reverend Dr. Stone
But the better times were all used up
And the worse times took control
Then drinkin' took my Walter
May the Lord protect his soul

Alone with two young kids to raise
Out on the Western plains
My children harmonized with wolves
And sang just like the rain
But haulin' hay and water
Were the desperate daily facts
Now the years have carved their memories
In the muscles of my back

Then I married for convenience sake
A blacksmith from in town
A half-breed name of Charlie Hawk
Who'd court me on his rounds
But he pawed me like a wolverine
And there was cheatin' in his blood
He fell upon my butcher knife
And crawled off through the mud

No one seemed to notice
When old Charlie disappeared
Me and them poor children
Never shed one single tear
We can run this place all on our own
Don't need no drunks or cheats
And the men all step aside now
When I walk down Market Street

This land was conquered by brave men
Your history books will say
Proud men upon fast horses
Drove the Indian away
My name is Hallie Lonnigan
And I'll have you all to know
That the secret of our History's
In a working woman's soul

Excerpted from Song of the West, *published by* HMG/Hightone Records, 1997.

THE COWBOY'S REPLY

Wallace David Coburn

Old and blemished and flecked with gray,
   A cow-horse feebly stands,
A weak reminder of the day
   He smote the desert sands
With flying hoofs that held the speed
   Of wings or prairie wind,
The model of a noble breed,
   His equal hard to find.

But e'en as since the world began,
   The march of Father Time
Has spared not beast nor even man,
   But passeth on sublime;
Hence, burdened with a score of years,
   The old horse bravely stands,
No more he'll chase the long-horned steers
   Across the prairie sands.

His head drops low, a mist bedims
   That eye once full of pride;
A tremor passes through his limbs,
   His age he cannot hide.
But, hark! his cowboy owner speaks,
   With cold scorn in his words,
A flush of pride lights up his cheeks,
   And ill his wrath he curbs:

"No, stranger, not for all the wool
    That grows upon your bands,
Not even for your money, fool!
    Nor all your stolen lands,
Would I while able to draw breath
    Or pull a trigger straight,
Sell that old friend—I'd rather death
    Would hurry up my fate.

"So, pard, I laugh your bid to scorn!
    Your money you can keep!
For that old horse was never born
    To drive a band of sheep!"

Excerpted from Rhymes from a Roundup Camp,
1903, with illustrations by Charles M. Russell.

TALL IN THE SIDESADDLE

Gwen Petersen

Sidesaddle riding once was a must
For a lady in long-layered skirt,
With knee fitted over a cradling hook,
She mostly endured till it hurt.

In the East she was expert at riding to hounds
In habit and black derby hat;
A groom helped her mount with his hand on
    her rump,
(Of course she would never say that!).

If ever she tried to ride astride
There were gasps and glances askance;
In order to do so in practical garb,
She would have to wear—masculine pants!

Besides that, she'd loosen some organs inside
With a leg on each side of a beast,
For females, like mermaids, everyone knew
Had lower limbs all in one piece.

But then she went west where the living was rough
To see what the real cowboys do;
To ride like a pretzel was painful and tough,
And twisted her backbone in two.

So she hiked up her skirts and piled on her bronc—
Put a leg on each side of her saddle,
With yippie ki yi, she went searching the range
For cattle—astraddle her saddle.

History somehow fails to mention her name,
This woman who helped win the West
Though small, she was tall when she got on her horse,
And she rode and she roped with the best.

Excerpted from In the Sidesaddle, *published by
Ranch Country Publishing.*

CHAPTER 6

CHARACTERS

Almost every cowboy poem has a character at its heart. Not just a central character, per se, but that woman or man who is just so colorful that someone has to write about 'em. However, it can also be said that the poets in this chapter are the characters themselves! Whether they are a single-minded cowboy only willing to perform one job, a high-mountain camp cook, or the heroic "Clancy of the Overflow," characters are what hold a cowboy poem together.

THE OLD RANCH COOK

Jack Walther

The most important man on any ranch
No matter which way you look
Is the one working in the kitchen.
He's the man called the cook.

When the grub is warmed-over stew and such,
Then not served up quite right,
The whole crew is grouchy and touchy.
They will be more or less on the fight.

When the grub is lots of steaks and gravy
With good fruit pies for dessert, too,
Seems the whole ranch runs smooth as silk.
You will have a happy, satisfied crew.

Such a good cook was Jim Dacer—
He could make the whole ranch just sing.
Good natured, right there on the job
From summer, year 'round into spring.

When a man had his personal problems
He would talk them out with old Jim
And go away feeling happy again
Like the whole world was right with him.

For years he held down the cook job,
Honest, faithful and true.
No matter what the challenge,
He seemed to know just what to do.

Guess we sort of took him for granted
Like he would always be there.
That his good meals and good nature
Were something we could depend on to share.

One morning, extra early, we had breakfast
Then saddled up and rode far away
To gather cattle on distant ranges.
It was late when we got back that day.

There were no lights in the kitchen.
The old dinner bell did not gong.
We went to check out the situation,
Knowing something was terribly wrong.

The horror and shock that hit us
As we entered that room,
We could not believe what we were seeing,
The way old Jim had met his doom.

It appeared a heart attack had hit him.
He died, sudden and still.
Then, as he collapsed that morning,
His body fell over the grill.

All day over that hot grill he had lain.
He was cooked clear through, you might know.
For such a good cook as he was,
What a horrible way he should go.

We buried him at sunrise next morning
On the sunny slope of a hill.
A meadowlark sang him a song
While the rest of the world was still.

We put up a headstone for him
That caught the rays of the morning's first sun.
Just his name, Jim Dacer—the date—
And below that it said, "Well Done."

Excerpted from Ruby Mountain Rhymes,
self-published, 1987.

COOK'S REVENGE

Ray Hanzlik

The snow had long since melted
And the prairie had turned green
When Turkey-Track's chuckwagon
And their riders hit the scene.

The cook drove his chuckwagon
Out across the rollin' plain
And parked on a gentle knoll
Just in case that it might rain.

Because just the night before
Lightning struck a long-horned steer
His scorched and bloated body
Sure filled some cowboys with fear.

A mile south of Sulphur Creek
As the foreman gave the word
On that flat, open prairie
Was the place they'd hold the herd.

After he parked the wagon
This gruff, grizzly little man
His Dutch ovens were dug in
Part of the cook's careful plan.

The hands bully-ragged the cook
And complained about the grub.
If he made one small mistake
He was bound to get the rub.

They complained about the beans,
And the burned cornbread, as well.
And chided him by sayin'
"It's a steak we'd like to smell."

Then, just like magic
He fried up some fresh beef steak
And brown gravy on biscuits
Made them do a double-take.

They praised his cookin' loudly
And no complaints could be heard
And they were prompt to chow-line
When returning from the herd.

They branded there for three days
And each day he served them steak
So those boys were all happy
In spite of scorched Johnny-cake.

Then it was time to move on
To gather another herd.
The cook packed up his wagon
As he smiled without a word.

He moved on to Red Owl Creek
Nearly thirty miles away
Had the coffee and beans cooked
By the twilight of the day

"It's back to baked beans and biscuits!"
One cowboy was heard to say.
"I know it won't be as good
As the steak of yesterday."

The next day was a tough one.
The cowboys were gettin' cross.
One said, "I'm so steak hungry,
I could damn near eat my hoss!"

Those cowboys cussed and pouted
And complained about the food.
They played mean tricks on the cook
And were in an ugly mood.

Those cowboys got to talkin'
Said they had all they could take.
So one up and asked the cook,
"Jist how come we cain't have steak?"

The cook, he sorta pondered,
Then he rubbed his bristled chin
And looked those boys in the face
With a twisted little grin

Said, "Too much steak might kill yuh,
And the change will do you good."
They growled and snarled at him
But his ground he firmly stood.

Then he really set 'em straight
When he said for all to hear,
"Why, it's thirty miles back to
That lightning-struck Longhorn steer."

Excerpted from Not All Cowboys Ride Horses, *published by The Livestock News.*

THE STAMPEDE AT JENNY'S CAFE

Chris Isaacs

I pulled in the other day at Jenny's,
A little cafe there in town.
Thought I'd get myself a tall iced tea
To help wash a burger down.

I was gettin' out of my ol' pickup
Contemplating a slice of apple pie,
When the cafe door slammed open,
And outside this feller flies.

He's wearing a helmet that looks like a mushroom,
And a pair of them Spandex pants;
He's got on one of them tank-top shirts,
Across the front it says "Viva la France."

Now, this ol' boy is airin' out his lungs,
And flappin' his arms about.
"Sacre bleu, vous êtes fou,"
I think is what I heard him shout.

His ol' eyes are big as silver dollars,
And he's blowin' rollers through his nose.
He jumps on the back of this racin' bike
And down the road he goes.

I'm wonderin' "what in the world is goin' on?"
As he pedals on out of sight.
But a hand don't have to cut much sign
To know he's on the fight.

So I goes on in the door to Jenny's
And look all around the place,
But all I see is ol' Ed a-standin' there,
A look of puzzlement on his face.

I says, "Ed, what was that all about?
Seems that guy was on the hook."
Ol' Ed just shrugs his shoulders
And gives me this funny look.

He says, "Chris, I don't know what happened.
I just came in to get a bite to eat
When that feller comes through the door,
Goes to the counter and takes a seat.

"He opens up the menu
And starts gazin' at the fare;
He gets this funny look on his face
Then turns to me and stares.

"He says, 'Pardon, monsieur, my name is Pierre,
And I'm a stranger in your land.
Please explain to me this food called 'calf-fries.'
This term I do not understand.'

"So, figurin' I can educate this feller on cowboy ways,
I explain about mountain oysters and calf fries.★
Ol' Pierre, he nods his head politely,
But I'm reading disbelief there in his eyes.

"About then, Jenny comes over to take my order,
And she asks me what I needed.
I says, 'Jenny, I think I'll just have some *french fries.*'
And that's when ol' Pierre stampeded."

★*mountain oysters* and *calf fries* are two terms for the same
  thing: the "by-product" produced after male calves are
  castrated. These delicacies are deep fried and enjoyed in
  homes and restaurants found in cattle country across
  the West.

Excerpted from Rhymes, Reasons, and Packsaddle
Proverbs, *published by Cowboy Miner Productions.*

CLANCY OF THE OVERFLOW

A. B. "Banjo" Paterson (1864–1941)

I had written him a letter which I had,
    for want of better
Knowledge, sent to where I met him
    down the Lachlan, years ago;
He was shearing when I knew him,
    so I sent the letter to him,
Just 'on spec,' addressed as follows:
    "Clancy, of the Overflow."

And an answer came directed
    in a writing unexpected,
(And I think the same was written
    with a thumbnail dipped in tar);
'Twas his shearing mate who wrote it,
    and verbatim I will quote it:
"Clancy's gone to Queensland droving,
    and we don't know where he are."

In my wild erratic fancy,
    visions come to me of Clancy
Gone a-droving "down the Cooper"
    where the Western drovers go;
As the stock are slowly stringing,
    Clancy rides behind them singing,
For the drover's life has pleasures
    that the townsfolk never know.

And the bush hath friends to meet him,
    and their kindly voices greet him
In the murmur of the breezes and the river on its bars,
And he sees the vision splendid
    of the sunlit plains extended,
And at night the wondrous glory
    of the everlasting stars.

I am sitting in my dingy, little office, where a stingy
Ray of sunlight struggles feebly down
    between the houses tall,
And the foetid air and gritty of the dusty, dirty city
Through the open window floating,
    spreads its foulness over all.

And in place of lowing cattle,
    I can hear the fiendish rattle
Of the tramways and the buses
    making hurry down the street,
And the language uninviting
    of the gutter children fighting,
Comes fitfully and faintly
    through the ceaseless tramp of feet.

And the hurrying people daunt me,
    and their pallid faces haunt me
As they shoulder one another
    in their rush and nervous haste,
With their eager eyes and greedy,
    and their stunted forms and weedy,
For townsfolk have no time to grow,
    they have no time to waste.

And I somehow rather fancy
    that I'd like to change with Clancy,
Like to take a turn at droving
    where the seasons come and go,
While he faced the round eternal
    of the cashbook and the journal—
But I doubt he'd suit the office,
    "Clancy, of the Overflow."

BANJO, MAY I HAVE THIS DANCE

Marion Fitzgerald

Banjo, may I have this dance,
Will you lead me in the waltz
To the rhythm of the hoofbeats
Of that Snowy Mountain horse,
Where courage rides as high
As the Kosciuszko peaks,
And the pride of that pony
Is dancing in my feet.
Twirl me in the twilight
Where the air is crystal clear,
To the swirling of the stockwhip
That echoes through the years,
And though my feet may wander,
And to other lands may roam,
The firelight on the flintstones
Will always dance me home.

Romance me 'cross the plains
Where Clancy's gone a-droving,
Where city life's a memory
And, with you, my heart is roving.
With cattle down the Lachlan,
Or the Cooper, let us ride
Towards the vision splendid
In those endless western skies.
Lead me with your lyrics
Where the kindly voices are,
And at night, we'll touch the tips
Of the everlasting stars.
And should ever my heart be hardened,
Your words will be my lure
To the freedom of the outback,
Where my heart will find a cure.

Embrace me in the verse
Of those bush songs that you've penned;
You're the singer, untouched by time,
Of the bush, my eternal friend.
Take me to the billabong,★
In Coolibah★ shade I'll lie,
Dreaming of that swaggie★
Beneath our Southern sky;
Where I can hear him singing,
It's haunting me, his song . . .
Although a century has passed,
It still makes a nation strong.
Oh, let me be your Matilda,★
Come, take me by the hand,
And waltz me, Banjo, waltz me,
Right across this great, great land.

★*billabong:* a water hole

★*Coolibah:* a native Australian eucalyptus tree

★*swaggie:* Aussie equivalent of the American "hobo"

★*Matilda:* swag carried over the shoulder

*Marion Fitzgerald writes here of Banjo Paterson,
Australia's best-loved poet of yesteryear and author
of the nation's unofficial theme song, "Waltzing
Matilda." Excerpted from* Snapshots of a Country
Girl, *self-published.*

SHARE AND SHARE ALIKE

Howard Parker

He'd never known no quittin' time
Just worked from sun to sun.
Then when the days got shorter
He would labor till he got done.

Now this is really somethin'
That I'd never seen before—
A cup of coffee in his hand
And his boots there on the floor.

His feet propped up and all laid back,
With the paper on his knee.
And the clock upon the mantel said
Fifteen minutes after three.

He said, "You know, the other day
I had to make a trip to town,
To visit with the banker,
cattle prices being down.

"I got there pretty early,
But the doors were locked up tight.
The curtains pulled, the lights turned off,
Not a person was in sight.

"Well, then, I got to thinkin',
On my weary homeward road,
How the bank owns one-third of what I've got,
But I'm packin' all the load.

"So, I give it hell till 3 o'clock,
Then I think it's only fair,
They send some gunsel* out from town
To handle the bank's share."

*gunsel: derived from a sailor's term for someone
who claims to have knowledge or expertise in doing
something, but is not the expert that he claims. This
differs from a "dude," who admits his inexperience.

Excerpted from Poetry and Prose from Horsethief
Crossing, *self-published, 1997.*

VIEJOS

Bill Wood

At the base of the Sierras,
In the foothills of those mountains
Where the waters of Kaweah, Kern,
And Tule swiftly flow,
In the mists of early morning,
While the blacktail deer are feeding,
You can almost hear the old ones,
As they tell of long ago.

You can see the cattle grazing,
Hear the quail softly calling,
You can smell the scent of white oak
Mingled strong with wild oats.
And the granite smells so pungent
That it's etched deep in your memory,
Like the vision of the redbud,
All arrayed in crimson cloak.

How my memories often haunt me
With the days that my past left me.
Though this book is not yet written,
One more chapter has been closed.
And I find that in my musings,
I often go back searching,
Through the voices of *viejos*
That now lie in deaf repose.

How I miss my old compadres,
How I long to hear those stories.
There was music in our laughter
To revive a weary hand.
There was knowledge in their tales,
And wisdom for the gleaning.
Paid for with the heavy price
Of the sweat and blood of man.

One day if God is willing,
Then I will be *Viejo*.
That causes me to wonder,
Will there be someone who dares
To keep alive traditions,
Place value in the old ways,
Who'll live their life undaunted,
By this modern world's affairs?

*This poem is a tribute to the wise old men
(the* viejos) *of early California, whose traditions
and style of horsemanship still have influence.*

TEXAS BRAGGIN'

Andy Hedges

On a roundup in the spring way back in eighty-two,
A Texas man was ridin' with some northern buckaroos.
Now this Lonestar cowboy was just what you'd expect,
From any Texas puncher with a lick of self-respect.
He'd say, "In Texas everything's a whole lot better
    and bigger.
The punchers all are punchier and as near as I can
    figure,
The horses all run faster, the cattle all are tougher,
The rivers all run wider and the work's a whole lot
    rougher."

Well, he commenced to braggin' every day of
    every week
Till it riled them buckaroos just to hear him speak.
And after talkin' it over they came to decide,
They'd have to somehow damage this braggin' cow
    boy's pride.
And since he'd said them Texans were so tough,
They'd have to pull a trick to call this puncher's bluff.
So, one day while they was fordin' a river, they
    happened to come across
A bunch of snappin' turtles a-hidin' in the moss.
Well, they put them turtles in his bedroll and threw
    it back in the wagon,
Figured that'd stop his never-ending braggin'.

So, that night when he got his bedroll out and laid
it on the ground,
Them buckaroos all walked over and they kinda
gathered 'round
To watch him stick his feet down in that roll,
A-thinkin' it would be a pretty funny show.
And sure enough, he stuck his feet in and he jerked
'em right back out,
And he kinda had a surprised look upon his snout.
When he flipped the bedroll open and he yelled
out to the crew,
"Well, looky there, boys . . . bedbugs! and little bitty
ones, too!"

Excerpted from the CD Days and Nights Spent in the Saddle, *self-published, 2001.*

GRANDPA'S EARLY MORNIN'S

Gary McMahan

Grandpa was a rancher. He come from the old school.
"The earlier the better" was his cardinal rule.

He'd roust us kids up in the middle of the night
"Rise and shine, girls!" he'd yell as he'd blind us
    with the light.

And if you didn't want your bed tipped over on
    your head,
you'd get your tail a movin' and do exactly what
    he said.

He'd pour a pot of strong coffee down us even tho'
    we's only sprouts,
then kick us out in the dark to try and find our
    mounts.

We'd stumble around his frozen corral, the stars
    a-shinin' bright.
To tell whose horse was which, you had to use a
    flashlight.

With jokes and quips he'd try to quell our early
    morning ire,
then haul us out to some distant pasture and light a
    sagebrush fire.

We'd huddle round that fire and shake till our
    bones would rattle,
not sure if it was the coffee, the cold, or dreadin'
    Grandpa's raunchy cattle.

We'd wait around there for what seemed like
    a week,
'til it was light enough to ride for these cows we
    was to seek.

I've never been as miserable my entire life
    combined
as I was out there with Grandpa on those early
    mornin' rides.

And whether he was right or wrong ain't for me
    to say,
but mornin's have been plumb tolerable since
    Grandpa passed away.

Excerpted from Gary McMahan in Poetry and Song,
published by Record Stockmen Press, 1997.

SECOND THOUGHTS

Pat Richardson

He was all propped up on pillows—
    y' could tell he was in pain.
There was hoses hooked t' bottles—
    drippin' slowly in his veins.
I said, "What would you do different,
    if y' done 'er all again?"
He pondered on the subject some an' sez,
    "That all depends.

"If the same thing was t' happen—
    an' I knew in advance—
I'da took along a rifle—an' an extra pair of pants.
I wouldn't have rode that gray horse,"
    he said deep in thought.
"An' in retrospect, I reckon,
    I'da shot that dog I brought.

"He's the cause of most my problems,"
    he sez with an icy stare.
"What the hell was he thinkin' of,
    barkin' at that bear?"
His nostrils flared in anger,
    he was twitchin' in his cast.
"An' any horse but that gray one—
    I needed one that's fast.

"He knew that bear was back there—
    he chased us down the hill.
I bailed off an' ran right past him,
    like he was standin' still.
An' I wouldn'ta climbed that oak tree,
    if I'd knowed at the time,
but no one ever told me that
    a grizzly bear could climb.

"I doubt I'da spurred his head so hard
    when he come climbin' close.
Of all the things I done,
    I b'lieve that pissed him off the most.
But the main thing I'd do different,
    if just one thing I could pick,
is I'da just stayed in the bunkhouse,
    an' pretended I was sick."

THE PERFECT TOOL

Darrell Arnold

If you've got work you're needin' done,
There is no doubt that I'm the one,
But I obey one sacred rule—
My hand has got to fit the tool.

My hand, by some genetic flaw,
Will not hold shovel, axe or saw.
And neither will a brace and bit,
Nor hammer, wrench, or auger fit.

I'm plenty smart, it sure ain't that,
There's lots of brain pow'r in this hat.
It's just that I prefer to grope
A twisted twine or rawhide rope.

What kind of work? Just anything,
As long as it requires this string
That I've got coiled here on this kack,
And me upon my horse's back.

I will admit (it's no big news)
There's other tools that I can use—
My cuttin' knife don't have no rust
And brandin' irons, yes, if I must.

But horseback work is where I shine
In desert, plains or timberline.
With rope in hand, I'm speakin' true,
There ain't no work that I won't do.